SPIRITUAL SUNLIGHT FOR THE WEARY

SPIRITUAL SUNLIGHT FOR THE WEARY

MEDITATIONS FOR THE CHRONICALLY FATIGUED

Lynn Vanderzalm

Harold Shaw Publishers
Wheaton, Illinois

© 1998 by Lynn Vanderzalm

ISBN 0-87788-823-X

Edited by Joan Guest

Cover design by David LaPlaca

Library of Congress Cataloging-in-Publication Data

Vanderzalm, Lynn.
    Spiritual sunlight for the weary : meditations for the chronically fatigued / by Lynn Vanderzalm.
      p. cm.
    ISBN 0-87788-823-X
    1. Chronic fatigue syndrome—Patients—Prayer-books and devotions—English.   I. Title.
    BV4910.335.V36 1998
    242'.4—dc21

                                                            98-23003
                                                            CIP

03 02 01 00 99 98
10 9 8 7 6 5 4 3 2 1

Acknowledgments

The following Bible versions are used in these meditations. Acknowledgment is gratefully made to the publishers for permission to use their copyrighted material:

NLT   Taken from the *Holy Bible*, New Living Translation, copyright © 1996. Used by permission of Tyndale House Publishers, Inc., Wheaton, Illinois 60189. All rights reserved.

NIV   Taken from the HOLY BIBLE, NEW INTERNATIONAL VERSION®. Copyright © 1973, 1978, 1984 by International Bible Society. Used by permission of Zondervan Publishing House. All rights reserved.

    The "NIV" and "New International Version" trademarks are registered in the United States Patent and Trademark Office by International Bible Society. Use of either trademark requires permission of International Bible Society.

KJV   Taken from *The King James Version* of the Bible.

NASB   Taken from the *New American Standard Bible*, © 1960, 1962, 1963, 1968, 1971, 1972, 1973, 1975, 1977 by The Lockman Foundation. Used by permission.

NCV   Taken from *The New Century Version*, © Word Publishing, Irving, Texas. Used by permission.

NKJV   Taken from *The New King James Version*. Copyright © 1979, 1980, 1982, Thomas Nelson Inc., Publishers.

NRSV   Taken from the New Revised Standard Version Bible, copyright © 1989 by the Division of Christian Education of the National Council of the Churches of Christ in the U.S.A. Used by permission. All rights reserved.

PHILLIPS   Reprinted with permission of the Macmillan Publishing Company, Inc., from the *New Testament in Modern English*, Revised Edition by J.B. Phillips, © J.B. Phillips, 1958, 1960, 1972.

TEB   Taken from *The Everyday Bible*, copyright © 1987 by Worthy Publishing, Fort Worth, Texas 76137. Used by permission.

TEV   Taken from *Today's English Version (The Good News Bible)*, © 1966, 1971, 1992 American Bible Society. Used by permission.

Contents

Introduction: Rest for the Weary   11

1 Facing the Losses

Is There a Purpose to These
     Losses?   14
Learning to Receive   16
The Gain of Loss   18
I Remember When . . .   20
Will People Ever Understand?   22
Losing Our Pride   24
Loss and Anger   26
Let It Go!   28
Total Dependence   30
With Friends Like These, Who
     Needs Enemies?   32
Aliens in a Healthy World   34

2 Calming the Fears

Will This Fear Ever Go Away?   36
Fearing Relapse   38
What Can Calm My Anxiety?   40
What If?   42
Angry with God   44
When the Future Looks
     Uncertain   46
Afraid to Bother God   48
Even If . . .   50
All I Need   52
Waiting to Live   54
Don't Worry!   56

3 Keeping Perspective

Why Good People Suffer and
     Bad People Don't   58

The Point of Suffering 60

Job's Wise Silence 62

Seeing the Big Picture 64

Every Purpose 66

Stronger through Adversity 68

Mercy in the Sky 70

God's Presence in Pain 72

Real Treasure 74

Looking beyond What We Can See 76

Confidently Waiting 78

Why Am I Hidden? 80

4 Feeling Worthwhile

What Am I Worth? 82

Staying by the Stuff 84

Using an Empty Jar 86

Illness Gives Us Empathy 88

Just As I Am 90

Do I Have Significance? 92

God's Expectations of Us 94

With All My Strength 96

The Right Measuring Stick 98

The Worth of Suffering 100

Lord, I Want to Serve 102

5 Living with Questions

Why Did You Make Me Like This? 104

Forgive Them? 106

Why This Waste? 108

What Did I Do to Deserve This? 110

How Can This Experience Be Good? 112

All of Life's Answers Questioned 114

Receiving a Gift We Didn't Want 116

Why Doesn't God Do Something? 118

Can Any Good Come from
  This Illness?   120
Will I Be Single Forever?   122

6 Finding Strength

Rest for the Weary   124
Finding Strength in Weakness   126
Why Won't I Rest?   128
Content with Weakness?   130
Don't Despise Those Who Are
  Weak   132
Jesus Understands   134
The Fellowship of Suffering   136
Too Tired to Do the Job   138
Made More Sensitive   140
Strength for the Long Haul   142
Power to the Weary   144
Too Tired to Read the Bible   146

7 Clinging to Hope

Hope in God   148
Choose to Live   150
He Promises Peace   152
That Saved a Wretch like Me   154
Is There Someone Special for
  Me?   156
Laughter, the Natural Healer   158
Waiting on Him—Alone   160
Don't Give Up   162
Why the Little We Can Do Is
  Enough   164
Wrapped in God's Comfort   166
Follow the Son   168

Meet the Writers   171
Further Help with Your Fatigue   175

Introduction
Rest for the Weary

Are you tired? Weary? Fatigued?

Who isn't?

We live in a fast-paced society. We try to operate at full speed in order to take in all that life has to offer. But in the process we overdo and overextend ourselves. The result is that we wear down and wear out. The solution for many people is to pull back a little and get some rest. For many people, that's all it takes to bounce back.

Some people, however, find that their fatigue doesn't go away with a good night's sleep. Their fatigue may be the result of having an infection or taking a certain medication or living with a thyroid imbalance. Chronic fatigue affects all aspects of their lives. Maybe you are among that group of people.

Still another group of people live with fatigue that is so severe that they are debilitated and sometimes bedridden. Their fatigue is the result of illnesses like fibromyalgia, kidney or heart disease, multiple sclerosis, or other immune-system disorders. I am part of this group of people.

For the past ten years I have lived with an illness known as chronic fatigue and immune dysfunction syndrome (CFIDS, pronounced *see-fids*). Some people call it simply chronic fatigue syndrome. Exhaustion and fatigue have been my constant companions for years.

But God has been my companion, too, giving me strength in the midst of weakness. He has given me strength to bear lots of pain, strength to keep a family together, strength to battle discouragement, strength to face lots of questions that don't have easy answers, strength to be a mother to a young daughter who has the same illness, strength to keep going.

Sometimes God strengthened me through his Word. Often he did it through people who encouraged me, who helped to carry the load, or who walked the same valley with me.

The meditations in this book are written by men, women, and children who live with fatigue that is chronic, that is not resolved with a good night's sleep and a little rest.* These people are veterans of living with fatigue. They have spent years conserving their energy. They have a lot to teach us about dealing with the emotional and spiritual side of fatigue.

Their faith has been challenged as some have watched their careers die, their friends leave them, and their bodies be drained of energy. Their faith has taken on new dimensions as some face daily pain, sleep disorders, unrelenting bone weariness.

In these pages they offer perspective and insights about some questions we all ask:

Is God good?
Where do I find faith in the darkness?

*To learn more about these writers, see "Meet the Writers" at the end of the book.

Where do I find hope in the midst of the despair?
How do I calm my fears?
How can I keep perspective?

They also ask questions borne from their unique suffering:

What is the purpose of my suffering?
How do I endure the losses?
What do I do with all my questions?
What are my priorities when I have so little energy?
What am I worth if I can't live a full life?
Where do I find strength in weakness?

I'm so glad that God is not afraid of our questions. In fact, he often meets us at these tension points in our lives. In the midst of the stresses he reveals that he has come to be the answer to our questions, the strength in our weakness, the light in our darkness.

I pray that these meditations will not only speak to your personal battle with fatigue but will also bring you hope and comfort as you share in the experiences of these people who have found God's strength to be real in the midst of their weakness.

Is There a Purpose to These Losses?

 "And I will give you treasures hidden in the darkness—secret riches. I will do this so you may know that I am the Lord, the God of Israel, the one who calls you by name" (Isaiah 45:3, NLT).

Have you ever lost something, searched for it, and in so doing found some item of greater value? If you suffer from a condition that leaves you chronically fatigued, you probably have lost several things: your health, possibly your independence, maybe your job, and often your sense of identity.

When we lose our sense of identity, we ask ourselves, "Who am I?" Where should we go for the answer? The best place to go is *beyond* ourselves to God, who is the only one who can make sense out of our losses.

In the midst of the dark times of our lives, God says, "I will give you treasures hidden in the darkness." Then he goes on to tell us why he has hidden treasures for us in the dark experiences of our lives: so that we will know that he is the Lord, who calls us by name.

Could it be that God allows our losses in order to redirect our focus and activity from ourselves to him? Jesus said, "How do you benefit if you gain the whole world but lose your own soul in the process?" (Matt. 16:26, NLT). It's not that what we lost was necessarily wrong or bad for us, but just that God has something of *greater* value in store for us. Gaining a more intimate relationship with God through illness is more precious than all the status we could attain. A deeper intimacy with him brings new meaning to our lives. We no longer despair, asking, "Now who am I?" Instead we rejoice in learning who *he* is—the God who calls us by name.

What have you lost? God has a treasure for you to find. Are you ready to search?

Father, knowing you and accepting the salvation you offer us in Jesus Christ is more valuable than anything I could possess. As I accept my losses, help me to find the treasures you have hidden for me in the darkness. Amen.

—*mm*

Learning to Receive

"But Jesus said, 'Let her alone, why must you make her feel uncomfortable? She has done a beautiful thing for me. . . . She has done all she could. . . . I assure you that wherever the gospel is preached throughout the whole world, this deed of hers will also be recounted" (Mark 14:6-9, Phillips).

Many of us are happier in the giving role than the receiving role; we do not like to feel indebted to another and prefer the position of the blessed giver. Chronic fatigue forces us into the uncomfortable position of being the needy ones.

I found this especially difficult when, after a year of illness, my husband and I moved from Africa to America. I found myself surrounded by kind neighbors in our new home and was soon blessed with wonderful friends. However, I was terribly reluctant to ask such new friends for help, and I felt uncomfortable when they offered. These people had never known me as the healthy, helpful giver, and I was not sure when I could return their kindness.

In a poignant scene from Mark 14, we find Jesus in a similar situation. He is passing through Bethany on his way to Jerusalem when a woman, whom he does not appear to know, tenderly anoints him with expensive perfume. Instead of joining in the admonitions of his disciples, who focus on the extravagance of the gesture and how the perfume should have been sold to feed the poor, Jesus surprises everyone by saying, "She has done a beautiful thing to me."

Here, our Lord shows us how to receive: graciously, openly, and without worrying about how or when we can return the kindness. When he honors the woman by saying that her gesture will be told all over the world, he reminds us that others are blessed when we allow them to minister to us. He shows us that when giving and receiving are carried out with love, they are really one and the same.

Lord, thank you for giving me a heart that wants to give, but forgive me for my pride, for keeping score when others offer help and kindness. Help me to follow your example of how to receive graciously. Help me to remember that in receiving what others give to me, I am allowing them to receive your blessing. Amen.

—lvv

The Gain of Loss

"What is more, I consider everything a loss compared to the surpassing greatness of knowing Christ Jesus my Lord, for whose sake I have lost all things. I consider them rubbish, that I may gain Christ" (Philippians 3:8, NIV).

One thing that people who are burdened with constant fatigue must face is that we are different from how we used to be. In many cases, we have lost our active lives. Some have lost relationships, status, and even jobs—things that had shaped us and had helped us to determine who we were. We have often experienced drastic changes in our lifestyles, and those changes sometimes cause our images of ourselves to become greatly distorted or damaged. This sense of loss can be overwhelming.

The apostle Paul understood what it meant to have a confidence based on status. As a purebred Hebrew of the tribe of Benjamin and as a religious zealot, he had been a prominent figure among his people and had been highly esteemed by his peers. While he knew that his credentials and life position made him a valuable person, he considered it a blessing to have lost all of the things that had been so significant to him and had made him important. He realized that his relationship with Jesus Christ mattered more than his worldly position. His relationship to Christ was the one thing that truly gave him self-worth.

As we live each day with the memory of our old lives, we do not have to be sad or confused about who we are now. We can live with the losses and realize that if they propel us to Christ, then we have gained a great deal more than we have lost. If we use this time of loss to seek to know Jesus Christ in a more intimate way—by spending time with him in prayer and in reading his Word—then we will come to the point of considering our losses to be gains too.

Dear Lord, when I feel an overwhelming sense of loss because of what this illness has robbed me of, help me to find my sense of self-worth in you. Remind me to understand my position in your kingdom. Help me to see this loss as a gain because through it I can choose to depend on you more fully. Amen.

—cs

I Remember When . . .

"As the deer pants for streams of water,
  so I long for you, O God.
I thirst for God, the living God.
  When can I come and stand before him?
Day and night, I have only tears for food,
  while my enemies continually taunt me, saying,
  'Where is this God of yours?'

My heart is breaking
  as I remember how it used to be:
I walked among the crowds of worshipers,
  leading a great procession to the house of God,
singing for joy and giving thanks—
  it was the sound of a great celebration!

Why am I discouraged?
  Why so sad?
I will put my hope in God!
  I will praise him again—
  my Savior and my God!" (Psalm 42:1-5, NLT).

The writer of this psalm, perhaps in exile far from home, remembers how it used to be, how he was able to worship God openly. But he misses the way it used to be. He would like his life back. He would like to worship God in the same way and in the same place as he had been able to do before. His enemies taunt him that his God is not acting on his behalf. "Where is your God?" they say.

"I remember when I used to be able to . . ." "I wish I could . . ." Do you find yourself saying things like this? Are you discouraged at the changes fatigue has forced on your life? Do you wish you could have your other life back? Do you wonder if God is with you?

God's answer to despair is always to hope in him. It is not just hope that things will get back to where they were before or that someday we will not be as sick as we are now—although there is nothing wrong in asking for that. But our hope is in God himself.

The results of this kind of trust in our Savior and Lord is that we will be able to praise God. Even if our circumstances do not change. Yes, even if we never recover from the situation that has caused our fatigue and illness.

God of Hope, take my despair and exchange it for your love. Teach me about hope in you, not just relief from my fatigue. Amen.
—hg

Will People Ever Understand?

 "He was despised and rejected—a man of sorrows, acquainted with bitterest grief. We turned our backs on him and looked the other way when he went by. He was despised, and we did not care" (Isaiah 53:3, NLT).

Do you find people accepting of your fatigue? Do they take you seriously, or do they say things like, "Well, you *look* good," implying that you must be exaggerating your symptoms and that it cannot be as bad as you say it is?

That is discouraging. It is hard when our friends and family members do not understand the degree to which our fatigue can be debilitating. So to avoid needing to explain for the tenth time just how awful we feel, we say, "I'm doing okay." That answer satisfies the other person, but it sure leaves us feeling disconnected and lonely.

The Lord has listened to my sobs over this many times. It is hard to deal with other people's inability to understand.

I find comfort in remembering that Jesus went through the very same thing. From the time he was born, he was misunderstood. People expected a king, and though Jesus was a king, he certainly did not *look* like one! Not even his own family understood him. When Jesus told the truth about who he was—the Son of God—people challenged him. Worse than that, they falsely accused him of blasphemy and crucified him.

Jesus knows exactly how it feels to be misunderstood. He knows the power of hurtful words. When Jesus was challenged, the Scriptures say that "he did not open his mouth" (Acts 8:32, NLT). Following his example, we do not have to defend ourselves if people are not willing to listen. Instead we can take comfort in knowing that the Lord is our defender and friend. He knows us, and he understands us.

Lord, the misunderstanding you suffered on my behalf is so much more severe than anything I have experienced. Thank you that you were willing to go through all of that pain and humiliation and rejection for me. Give me your grace as I deal with people who do not understand my situation and who say hurtful and thoughtless things. Amen.

—*mm*

Losing Our Pride

 "Remember how the Lord your God has led you in the desert for these forty years, taking away your pride and testing you, because he wanted to know what was in your heart. He wanted to know if you would obey his commands" (Deuteronomy 8:2, NCV).

The fatiguing illness with which I have struggled since I was a teenager has taken many things away from me: the chance to go to college, the chance to be involved in productive work, the chance to live on my own. The physical strength and stamina I once had are gone. I have been reduced to a person who is dependent on parents and friends for many of the things I had hoped to do for myself by the time I was in my mid-twenties.

Independence and self-reliance are not bad things for a person to have. Neither are the physical strength and stamina that underpin them. But often, when these things are stripped away, we lose something else—pride.

Pride is a good thing to lose. With it we feel strong, capable, and wholly self-sufficient. We feel deserving of the blessings that come our way. We see what we have accomplished, and we forget God's role in our success. Pride breeds a sense of self-adequacy.

Even though being stripped of pride is disconcerting, it can bring us closer to God. He can work with a humble heart. God wants us to be aware of our need for him, and he wants us to rely on his strength.

Perhaps your hardships, while they have been painful, have been God's instrument to bring you closer to him. He has used some fire to purify you, make you more dependent on his strength, more patient for his timing, and more reliant on his grace. Maybe that is not such a loss after all.

Dear God, help me to realize that all my losses are not without great gain. Thank you for showing me that in the stripping process you have also made me stronger in some areas of life. Give me a humble heart. Help me rely on you, not myself. Amen.

—*cm*

Loss and Anger

"The Lord will comfort Israel again and make her deserts blossom. Her barren wilderness will become as beautiful as Eden—the garden of the Lord. Joy and gladness will be found there. Lovely songs of thanksgiving will fill the air" (Isaiah 51:3, NLT).

Desert. Barren wilderness. That is what I felt like after I became ill with chronic fatigue and immune dysfunction syndrome. I had been a practicing portrait artist when my exuberant, enthusiastic spontaneity came to an abrupt halt with the sudden onset of the illness.

My life changed in so many drastic ways, and they all seemed negative. I was no longer able to be involved in normal social gatherings. I lost my earning ability. I lost the sense of worth from community or peer recognition. I lost my ability to keep a clean house or to shop for my own groceries. All these things, which I had enjoyed for most of my life, were no longer options for me. The absence of those activities created a wilderness, a wasteland.

The other kind of desert I have experienced in a more ongoing way is the white heat of volatile anger. I feel so violently mad about being held captive by my body and its limitations. Sometimes the anger sears, like a fish on the grill. Sometimes the anger intensifies in a deep aloneness.

I have been sick for many years now, and the Lord has repeatedly used this promise from the book of Isaiah to comfort me. I hope that it gives you comfort too. In the verse he promises to take the deserts and wilderness areas of our lives and turn them into a paradise, a garden in which he will dwell, a garden in which will be heard songs of thanksgiving and gladness. That is a powerful promise.

The verse clearly indicates that it is the Lord who will comfort us and restore our deserts to gardens of joy. Even in the burning, devastating moments, we can look forward to the time when he will transform this wilderness into a place of beauty. God will not leave us in the wilderness of our despair, but he will bring us to the oasis of thanksgiving and joy.

Thank you, restoring Father, that nothing is wasted with you! Please help me to remember what you have shown me in the past and to keep expecting to find your comfort, joy, and gladness—even in dry places. Amen.

    —*bsm*

Let It Go!

 "I am still not all I should be, but I am focusing all my energies on this one thing: Forgetting the past and looking forward to what lies ahead, I strain to reach the end of the race" (Philippians 3:13-14, NLT).

After having spent seventeen years on the mission field, my husband and I had to face the grim reality that my illness would not let us continue to live overseas. Our world spun into disorder as we sold and packed our belongings and said our good-byes. The magnitude of the loss was overwhelming.

During those months, God's voice kept saying to me, "Let it go!" I knew that he was right, but I found letting go to be a difficult process. I was afraid that if I let go of the good experiences and ministry he had given me, I would be left empty-handed.

In his letters to a chronically ill member of the court of Louis XIV, François Fénelon—a seventeenth-century spiritual director—counseled "that what we weep for would have made us weep eternally. What we believe to have lost was lost when we thought we had it. God has taken it into safe keeping to give it back to us soon in the eternity which draws near."

When we consider or count something lost, we should not passively resign ourselves to losing it; we should actively surrender it. Through the slow—and usually painful—process of detachment, we have the opportunity to cooperate actively with God and what he is doing through the details and milestones of our life. Because of this, even our illness, which we did not ask for, can become an offering to the Lord. Our deepening relationship with our Lord Jesus Christ depends on our willingness to let go of the past. The ministries, activities, and even friends whom we love must be given back to God, who will replenish the vacuum they have left with an ever-growing relationship with him. And in his time, God will return to us that which we have lost.

I am willing to let go of the past that I cherish so deeply, dear Lord, because I love you more than my past. Lead me on toward knowing you better. I choose to count everything worthless compared to the joy of knowing you as my Lord and Savior. Amen.

—*ph*

Total Dependence

 "I am the vine, you are the branches. Those who abide in me and I in them bear much fruit, because apart from me you can do nothing. Whoever does not abide in me is thrown away like a branch and withers; such branches are gathered, thrown into the fire, and burned" (John 15:5-6, NRSV).

The fatiguing illness in my life took away my independence, and I am not always sure I like that. I liked being able to be active and to do things for myself. I liked being the person on whom others could depend for service, for getting a job done.

Debilitated by illness and fatigue, I am now the dependent one. I am dependent on other people—my family and friends—to do many things for me. I still bristle about that, thinking that it is not good to be dependent.

I realize now that I had come to believe that all dependence is bad. After studying Scripture, however, I realize that dependence is one of the qualities God *wants* us to have. He wants us to depend on him for our lives and our strength.

Before I faced this debilitation in my life, I must admit that I did not depend on God as I should have. I was busy *doing* instead of *abiding*. Being a wife, mother of four daughters, homeschool teacher, substitute Sunday school teacher, Junior Church assistant, Awana secretary, pianist for the Junior Choir and various other church ensembles kept my mind on myself and all of my responsibilities. Now I am *abiding* instead of *doing* because doing is out of the question.

Finally God has me in the place that he has always wanted me to be—totally dependent on him. I can choose to chafe against that realization, or I can rest in it, learning each day how to depend more fully on him. He wants me to be a branch that depends completely on him, the vine, for sustenance, nourishment, and strength.

Even though I cannot be doing all the things I could do before I became ill—things I thought would please God—I can be doing the thing he wants me to be doing at this stage of my life: abiding in him, totally.

Dear God, now that you have my full attention, help me to depend on you for all my needs. Help me to see this kind of dependence as a good thing, not something to be avoided. Amen.

    —*cf*

With Friends Like These, Who Needs Enemies?

 "People who are at ease mock those in trouble. They give a push to people who are stumbling" (Job 12:5, NLT).

If you suffer from crippling fatigue, you probably have had well-meaning people give you lots of advice. Maybe you have heard things like "If you just stay busy, you won't feel quite so bad" or "Maybe if your life had a bit more direction, you would have more energy" or "I always find that I feel better after I've had a good walk. You should try that too."

If you are like me, you would like to scream when people say these kinds of things. For many years during my battle with chronic fatigue and immune dysfunction syndrome, a "good walk" would have sent me into a crash that would have lasted for days or weeks.

But while I sometimes have felt that people who are at ease—those who may be completely healthy—have given me a push, I also realize that they say these insensitive things more out of ignorance than malice.

In the apostle Paul's letter to the Galatians, we see another response to people who are going through difficult illness: Paul says, "But even though my sickness was revolting to you, you did not reject me and turn me away. No, you took me in and cared for me as though I were an angel from God or even Christ Jesus himself" (Gal. 4:14, NLT). What a redeemed way to look at illness! Paul's experience both encourages and challenges me. It encourages me because it shows people responding in helpful ways to another person's sickness. It challenges me because my first response to people's trouble is not always a compassionate one.

Dear Lord, the Galatian church's loving response comforts me. Help me to imitate it rather than reflect complacent ease. And, Lord, I choose to forgive those who have been thoughtless and inconsiderate to me during my illness; I forgive them because you continue to forgive me. Thank you, Lord. Amen.
  —*bsm*

Aliens in a Healthy World

"All these people were still living by faith when they died. They did not receive the things promised; they only saw them and welcomed them from a distance. And they admitted that they were aliens and strangers on earth. . . . They were longing for a better country—a heavenly one" (Hebrews 11:13-16, NIV).

I sometimes feel as if I am an alien living in a healthy world. The people around me hurry to jobs, families, and social events. Meanwhile I have been confined to bed with disabling fatigue that makes me feel as if I have run a marathon when all I have done is walk to the bathroom. I feel lonely, confused, and exhausted. I often feel that I belong in another country—a country that would understand and empathize with my struggles or at least slow down a bit. I have lost my citizenship in normal life.

The people in this passage from Hebrews were called aliens because they knew their "real" home was in heaven, not on earth. They were searching for a better country—a heavenly one, a country without pain or death or persecution.

Imagine how much Jesus must have felt like an alien when he walked this earth. After all, he had already seen heaven. He must have been frustrated by the limitations of earth and the misunderstanding he faced. But he chose to use his time in this "foreign land" to reveal his Father's will to us.

As we live in a world that will not slow down to understand us, we, too, have a choice to make. We can choose to become angry that we are not out there with everyone else living the good life, or we can choose to use this time to draw nearer to God and reflect on who he is and what he has done for us.

Let's depend on God to restore us as we rest in him. Through this time of fatigue, we have been given the gift of being set apart because we are too tired to join everyday life. Let's choose to embrace the gift of time we have been given with thanksgiving.

Dear Lord, thank you for willingly becoming an alien on this earth for me. Help me to see this difficult time of debilitation as a gift. Thank you for loving me even when I feel like an alien. Amen.

—*dm*

Will This Fear Ever Go Away?

 "I prayed to the Lord, and he answered me, freeing me from all my fears. . . . The eyes of the Lord watch over those who do right; his ears are open to their cries for help" (Psalm 34:4, 15, NLT).

In a cold sweat I jolted upright! The clock beamed 2:00 A.M. In terror I cried, "O, dear God, *please* take away this awful fear. I can't take any more of these dreams." This one was about being at the ocean, and the waves were just about to engulf me.

When I awakened, I frantically took my Bible, which opened up to Isaiah 43:2: "When you go through deep waters and great trouble, I will be with you. When you go through rivers of difficulty, you will not drown!" (Isaiah 43:2, NLT). God used that verse to calm my fear and re-assure me of his presence. He promised to be with me in the deep waters of my nightmare as well as the deep waters of my life. He spoke to my need through his living Word.

The terrifying dream that night was not an isolated incident. I had been having lots of nightmares since I had been hospitalized and nearly died. The trauma had resulted in threatening dreams of dying.

But as I read the passage from Isaiah 43, I realized how personally God knew me. He knew every detail of my dream and used this specific passage to deliver me from my fear. I returned to a restful sleep.

Fear is not unique to me. All through Scripture we read: "Do not be afraid." God knows that it is human nature to fear, and thus he reassures us with a promise: "I will be with you."

What frightens you? Is it the possibility of becoming more physically limited and thus more dependent, or is it the increasing medical bills? Maybe it is the fear of death, as I experienced, or the fear of living *indefinitely* with chronic illness. Whatever the fear, God tells us that these situations will not drown us. He does not say that we will not die, for death is appointed to each of us in God's time. But he does promise to be with us as we go *through* the trials.

Dear Father, whether I am awake or asleep, you are constantly alert and attentive to my cries. What an assurance you give me that you not only *hear* me but also *deliver* me from my fear by the power of your living Word. Amen.
—*mm*

Fearing Relapse

 "When I am afraid, I will put my trust in Thee. . . . In God I have put my trust; I shall not be afraid" (Psalm 56:3-4, 11, NASB).

Ten years ago my life changed. One day I was fine, and the next day I was flat on my back with what I thought was a bad case of the flu. But it was not the flu. For the next six weeks I was so exhausted that I could not be on my feet long enough to fix dinner for my family.

Over a year's time, I slowly got better. Then, mysteriously, the illness disappeared. I was well for two years. I began to think that the illness was a thing of the past.

However, overnight, it returned again. At that point I was diagnosed with CFIDS. That was ten years ago, and since then the cycles of fatigue have become a part of my life.

Now when I have two bad days in a row, I find myself feeling fear. What if the terrible fatigue comes back? How bad will it be? How long will it last? What will happen to my life, my responsibilities, my plans? All of us who have known serious fatigue live with that fear lurking in our minds, ready to consume us if we do not choose to trust our future days to a loving God. What does trust in God look like? It is choosing to believe what God *says* is true in spite of what I *feel*.

The verses from Psalm 56 have encouraged me over the years. Some days, when fear comes out of nowhere or when I have a sudden energy drop, I need to fight to choose to believe that the God who is working in my life also loves me. Some days I need to work hard at trusting him with my future. Other days, I find that my trust and belief in God is strong and that the fear does not overwhelm me. The good news is that God, who knows me, has made provision for both kinds of fears: *himself.*

Tireless God, take my fear of the known and the unknown and replace it with yourself. Thank you for being a God I can trust. Amen.
    —*hg*

What Can Calm My Anxiety?

 "And His song will be with me in the night, a prayer to the God of my life" (Psalm 42:8, NASB).

When King Saul was troubled by an evil spirit, he called on David to play his harp. Causing the spirit to depart, the music refreshed and healed Saul. When my spirit is overwhelmed, music can also lift me above the darkness. When my mind is restless and overactive, music calms me. When my body is wrestling with pain, music soothes me. Music is a powerful healer.

Music can focus our thoughts on the truths of Scripture. When we are in the midst of difficulty, we can use the words of uplifting songs to help keep our thoughts on the reality of God's loving care. A hymn like "Hiding in Thee" assures us of God's protection. "Does Jesus Care?" reminds us of his tender love. "Abide with Me" assures us of his presence. I keep hymnbooks at home and often just read the words for encouragement. An enlarged print edition of the Psalms is my useful bedside companion. The words of the Psalms never fail to focus my thoughts on God's unfailing love and faithfulness.

Music can direct our thoughts away from the present circumstances. When the mind and other senses are occupied with music, the body is able to relax. When the body relaxes, pain is lessened. When the pain is lessened, the emotions are quieted. Gentle, soothing music can set in motion a positive physical response. Music does not need words to do this. In fact, simple solo instruments like the flute, harp, and guitar are the most calming. I made a recording of my favorite meditative music and use it for sleepless or pain-filled nights. My tape player and headphones help shut out other distracting sounds. I close my eyes and let the music seep into my soul, and I am comforted.

A few days before a friend died of cancer, I took my flute to play for her. She was in and out of consciousness, often very agitated; she complained she could see demons in the room. I began to play hymns while two other people softly sang. Immediately, my friend's tossing stopped. Her uncontrollable chattering quieted. Her anxious breathing slowed as she closed her eyes and listened, sometimes mouthing words along with us. I will never forget this testament to the power of song.

Lord, thank you for the blessing of music. Thank you for using it in my life as an instrument of peace and worship. Amen.

—rr

What If?

 "We demolish arguments and every pretension that sets itself up against the knowledge of God, and we take captive every thought to make it obedient to Christ" (2 Corinthians 10:5, NIV).

What if my health gets worse and I cannot work even part-time? What if I lose my job? What if I cannot pay the doctor's bills? What if we lose our medical insurance? What if we lose our house? What if I end up on the street or in a nursing home?

Have you ever caught yourself playing "what if"? It is a deadly game that magnifies your problems. Playing "what if" increases your anxiety, creates depression, tenses your muscles, and weakens your immune system.

The passage from 2 Corinthians 10 reminds us that God wants us to capture these negative thoughts, challenge them, and put them to death. What does it mean to do that? Capturing those negative thoughts means recognizing them for what they are; they are not reality but worst-case-scenario fears. Challenging those thoughts means recognizing that we do not have to believe them. We are not slaves to those thoughts; Scripture reminds us that we can take them captive.

Putting negative thoughts to death means replacing them with the truth. When your mind starts playing the "what if" game, play back—with the truth. Try confronting your negative "what ifs" with positive probabilities. What if God chooses to heal me (Ps. 103:3)? What if God promises strength in my weakness (2 Cor. 12:9-10)? What if God cares for me more than the birds outside my window (Matt. 6:25-26)? What if God says he will never, never forsake me (Heb. 13:5)?

Paul tell us in Philippians 4:8 that we can choose to have a positive, peaceful spirit. We can fill our minds with thoughts that are true, honorable, just, pure, lovely, and gracious. This kind of thinking quiets our hearts, produces joy, relaxes our muscles, and strengthens our immune systems. We do not have to be caught in a cycle of anxiety and depression. Peace is available if we choose it. God is in control.

Lord, even when my life seems out of control, I know that you hold all things in your hands. Help me to take my fears captive and practice telling myself the truth. Amen.

—TT

Angry with God

 "O Lord, I cry out to you. I will keep on pleading day by day. O Lord, why do you reject me? Why do you turn your face away from me? I have been sickly and close to death since my youth. I stand helpless and desperate before your terrors. . . . You have taken away my companions and loved ones; only darkness remains" (Psalm 88:12-18, NLT).

Have you been angry with God because of your illness and fatigue? Have you felt that he has abandoned you or rejected you? Maybe this plea from the psalmist is one you could have uttered. Maybe you feel that God has robbed you of your companions and loved ones and that only darkness remains.

If you have felt that hot anger toward God, what have you done with it? Have you voiced it to him? Have you voiced it to other people?

Many people feel guilty about feeling angry with God, thinking that they should never have those feelings toward God—certainly never say angry things to him. I am glad that the Scripture record includes the psalms, many of which are intense ragings against God. The psalms are full of accusations and questions and demands. In Psalm 88 the psalmist asks God why he has done certain things. The psalmist accuses God of taking away his friends and loved ones, leaving him only in darkness.

It appears that God can handle the psalmist's ragings. It appears that God does not condemn him for his anger.

I find these raging psalms comforting, in a way. They tell us that God does not expect that we will always be full of faith, always be full of praise, always have positive responses. They tell us that God accepts our range of emotions, from awe to anger. Maybe these psalms suggest that not only is it acceptable to express our anger in front of God but also that it is the *only* effective place to express it—to the God who knows us and loves us, to the God who can hear our anger and remind us that he has not abandoned us.

Dear God, sometimes I don't know what to do with the anger that wells up inside me. The helplessness I feel is overwhelming. Thank you that you allowed your people to rage at you and express their accusations. Thank you that you didn't condemn them for it. Thank you that you invite me to express all my fears and anger to you too. Amen.
    —lv

When the Future Looks Uncertain

 "So don't worry about tomorrow, for tomorrow will bring its own worries. Today's trouble is enough for today" (Matthew 6:34, NLT).

Before my illness struck, I had some fairly exciting plans for the future. I knew where I wanted to go and how I was going to get there. I had made careful plans and had stuck to them faithfully. I could not have been more ready.

Suddenly and without warning, I lost my health. It was something I never believed would happen to me. If the suffering was not enough to pull me down, my crumbling dreams were. I was veering off my road to somewhere and onto a road of uncertainty. Before I became ill, I had a specific itinerary, a destination. Now I felt like a wanderer—trying to get by.

Many troubling worries can surface when we suffer from a long-term illness. The future is definitely uncertain. Glossy plans may have to give way to a more precarious blueprint for survival. Previously, we may have felt in control of our future. Losing that feeling of control can lead to a fear of what will happen to us.

Worry is a waste of our time, and it dilutes our faith. It diverts our attention and energy from the present situation. When we worry, we do not put our assurance in God, who is capable of giving us what we need. Worry saps our strength, renders us inefficient, and destroys our faith. Worst of all, it depletes our joy, replacing it with a self-inflicted burden.

Sometimes we place our faith in things that have a limited power. Our faith should rest in the ultimate Power. Instead of relying on our own strength and abilities, we can rely on God to provide all our needs—now and in the future. We can replace our worry with faith, our self-sufficiency with a complete reliance on God, and our fear of an uncertain future with a peace and a calm.

Lord of the future, help me to trust in you alone to provide for my needs. Give me the strength not to worry. Give me faith in your providential care. Help me to rest day by day in your love for me. Amen.

—*cm*

Afraid to Bother God

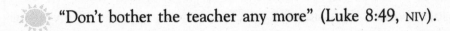 "Don't bother the teacher any more" (Luke 8:49, NIV).

Many of us can relate to the sick woman whose story is told in Luke 8. She had been ill for twelve years. Presumably, she had seen countless healers who promised relief, and she had tried all sorts of cures at great expense. But no one could help her.

The woman was desperate for help. Having heard of Jesus' reputation as a healer, she fought her way toward him despite the crushing crowds. Jesus was on his way to the home of Jairus, whose daughter was dying. We can well imagine the disciples' irritation with the crowds as they tried to clear a path for Jesus. Jairus was an important man, a ruler in the synagogue, and his daughter was desperately ill. The others must wait.

But when the woman reached out and touched the edge of Jesus' cloak, he suddenly stopped. "Who touched me?" he asked. After several tense moments, the woman finally confessed and told the crowd how she was healed the moment she touched him.

This story speaks not only of Jesus' all-encompassing power but also of his willingness and tireless ability to meet our needs. Despite the admonitions of those who had given up, saying, "Don't bother the teacher anymore," our Lord assures us in this story that he wants us to bother him. He is concerned about what concerns us, and he never grows weary or turns away when we reach out to him. No matter how often we turn to him, he will always stop and face us. Jesus is never too busy for us, and no heartfelt request is too trivial.

Lord Jesus, forgive me when I don't reach out to you, whether it's from fear or pride or lack of faith. Help me to pour out my heart to you when I'm hurting and trust you to hear my requests. Amen.
　　—lvv

Even If . . .

"Even though the fig trees have no blossoms, and there are no grapes on the vine; even though the olive crop fails, and the fields lie empty and barren; even though the flocks die in the fields, and the cattle barns are empty, yet I will rejoice in the Lord! I will be joyful in the God of my salvation" (Habakkuk 3:17-18, NLT).

When I was younger and had not yet experienced a lot of life's potholes, I believed that faith was a somewhat natural response. Now I know that faith most often is a deliberate choice, not a natural response. We must choose to believe that God is good, even if we feel that life is crumbling around us.

I saw this kind of faith powerfully demonstrated in a place I least expected it. Before I became ill, I traveled overseas with my husband to disaster sites that were served by the Christian relief agency for which he worked. In the mid-eighties we visited West Africa, which was in the throes of a severe drought and famine. We were there just after harvest, and the crop was very meager. Not only had the drought prevented the crops from growing very well, but the crops that did grow had been destroyed by swarms of locusts. Most families whom we visited had harvested only a few basketfuls of millet, barely enough to last them a month.

As I listened to a young farmer and church leader talk about the food shortage, I asked him, "How has all of this devastation affected the church? How has it affected your view of God?"

He looked at me strangely and replied, "Just because we don't have any food does not mean that God does not love us. God is good even if the rains don't come. God is good even if we don't have food."

This African's example of faith strengthened me years later when I was tempted not to rejoice in God's goodness because I was exhausted and my daughter was ill. I had to make a deliberate choice to trust God's goodness, even if we never recovered.

God's character does not change even if our circumstances do. We must be willing to trust him and rejoice in his goodness, even if our pain remains, even if we do not regain our physical strength.

Lord, I choose to rejoice in your goodness—even if I do not get better, even if I relapse. Give me strength to do that. Amen.

　　—lv

All I Need

 "You, Lord, are all I have, and you give me all I need; my future is in your hands. How wonderful are your gifts to me; how good they are" (Psalm 16:5-6, TEV).

Illness stripped my life of some significant things. It robbed me of physical stamina. Because I was couchbound, I lost my involvement in the ministries I felt God had given me to do. Whenever I left the house, even to attend a church service or take a very short ride in the car, I would become sicker and suffer a physical crash that would last for days. My relationships dwindled to the few people who would come to our house or to the people with whom I could talk on the phone.

In addition to these external losses, I felt as if I had been stripped of the things that gave me inner definition. I felt empty, as if there was nothing left of my life.

Maybe you have been at that point, too. If so, then you also may find comfort in the passage my husband shared with me one day. Into the midst of what I considered to be emptiness, the verses of this psalm helped me speak words of faith: "You, Lord, are all I have, and you give me all I need." Once I said those words, I realized that I had not been empty at all. God had always been there.

These words became a daily prayer, a confession of faith in the midst of the losses. I repeat them to the Lord when I first awaken in the morning to remind myself that even though I have lost many things, he has given me all I need.

Instead of focusing on what we have lost, we can affirm what we *have:* the Lord's faithful presence. We can also affirm that our future is in God's hands. The faithful God who made us and who has called us to himself holds our future in his loving hands. That is, indeed, all we need.

Lord, thank you for giving me yourself. Thank you that when I have your presence, I have all that I need. Thank you that I can put my past, present, and future in your loving hands. Amen.

—*lv*

Waiting to Live

"But I am trusting you, O Lord, saying, 'You are my God!'
My future is in your hands" (Psalm 31:14-15, NLT).

I have heard many teachings on the importance of learning to wait on
the Lord. But nothing prepared me for years of waiting to live. Chronic
fatigue so utterly dominated my life that during the first several years of
my illness I felt as if I were merely existing, not living. My circumstances were unspeakable, and I was in total agony. I was surviving,
waiting for the next day to bring some relief. But the relief did not
come. I could not think, could not read my Bible, and could not pray.
Breathing hurt, crying hurt, even moving my head hurt. This went on
month after month, year after year.

The excruciating pain that had such a stranglehold on my life
wasn't only physical. I had to wait to finish my education. I had to wait
to be involved in any type of ministry. I had to wait to attend church. I
even had to wait for years to marry the man I loved. Everything in my
life was put on hold!

It was during these dark times that I learned to trust God in a profound way. Even though I had no strength to function spiritually in any of the normal ways, for the first time in my life, my faith became very simple and clear. Everything that I believed and hoped for came down to one question: Did I trust God?

When our lives are reduced to the essentials of survival, we have a choice. Will we trust God with our future? Will we trust that he is good? Will we place our lives in his hands, even if that means we must wait years to see the unfolding of his plan?

Lord who holds me in your hands, take my life and use it for your good purposes. Sometimes it feels as if I am waiting to live. Help me to confidently wait on you, knowing that you love me and that you will be my hope and strength. Amen.

—sf

Don't Worry!

 "So I tell you, don't worry about everyday life—whether you have enough food, drink, and clothes. Doesn't life consist of more than food and clothing? Look at the birds. They don't need to plant or harvest or put food in barns because your heavenly Father feeds them. And you are far more valuable to him than they are. Can all your worries add a single moment to your life? Of course not" (Matthew 6:25-27, NLT).

Constant worry is a way of life for some people. There is even new evidence that some people have a genetic predisposition to worry. But regardless of whether or not you were born a worrier, chronic illness can make you one: *What if I never recover? What if they don't find a cure? What if I lose my job, my home, even my marriage? These are legitimate concerns, but ironically, fretting about them will only eat away at what little energy you have.*

Worry requires a great deal from us and gives nothing in return. As Jesus points out in Matthew 6, worry is essentially nonproductive.

He admonishes us to stop worrying and to use our energies instead to seek his kingdom. But how do we accomplish this?

In this same passage in Matthew, Jesus shows how our heavenly Father amply provides for the birds. Living day-to-day, they don't fret or worry, and God lavishly feeds and clothes them. So why can't we possess this simple peace of mind as the birds do? The answer, as Jesus points out, is our lack of faith. We simply do not trust God to meet our daily needs. We ignore the fact that he knows our greatest needs and cares about us. We ignore the fact that he meets these needs moment-to-moment while we focus on what might go wrong tomorrow. Like the pagans—those without a personal relationship with God—we run around despairing and fretting about nonessential things (Matt. 6:32).

And what is the antidote to worry? Not self-help books, support groups, or psychotherapy. Rather it is walking in the knowledge that God knows our needs and cares for us, and then trusting him to do what he has promised.

Heavenly Father, guard my heart and mind from worry, and strengthen my resolve as I daily put my trust in you. Forgive me for my weak faith. Help me to use my energy to seek your kingdom and your righteousness. Amen.
—lvv

Why Good People Suffer and Bad People Don't

 "I had almost lost my faith because I was jealous of proud people. I saw wicked people doing well. They are not suffering; they are healthy and strong. They don't have troubles like the rest of us; they don't have problems like other people" (Psalm 73:2-5, NCV).

Sometimes it is easy for those of us with chronic illnesses to look around us and come to the conclusion that life is not fair. We see people who do not love God or live by his commands, and they appear to be doing very well. They are healthy, and they prosper. What's more, they believe they do not need God and attribute their success to their own efforts. Conversely, many who do love God suffer hardships.

Why aren't the people who love God more successful? Why are their lives so hard?

Many people in our churches and Christian circles teach what could be termed a "prosperity gospel," which suggests that all we need to do is become a Christian, give more, or do something for God. In return, he will make all our problems disappear. We will be healthy and prosperous, and our lives will be easy. It is a spiritual philosophy of "give to get." All that we get is attributed to our spiritual adequacy.

This perspective is contrary to what Jesus taught when he said, "But the gate that opens the way to true life is very small. And the road to true life is very hard" (Matt. 7:14, TEB). He makes it clear that following him may cost us a lofty position here on earth instead of guarantee us prosperity (see Matt. 10:16-23).

No amount of material things, health, or prosperity can equal the joy that comes from Christ. The material things can never build character and strength. They are temporary. When we look with bitterness and jealousy on people who are more prosperous than we are, it only keeps us from taking advantage of what God has given us. "Yet what we suffer now is nothing compared to the glory he will give us later" (Rom. 8:18, NLT).

Dear God, help me to remember that while the road you have given me is hard, you have promised to give me strength for enduring these trials. Help me to be sure of my own heart instead of judging those around me. Amen.

—cm

The Point of Suffering

 "This suffering is all part of what God has called you to. Christ, who suffered for you, is your example. Follow in his steps" (1 Peter 2:21, NLT).

During the long years of living with a fatiguing illness, I have found great comfort from the writings of suffering saints. The writings of Elisabeth Elliot, Tim Hansel, Diane Diebler Rose, Jen Larcombe, and Sheila Walsh have given me courage and perspective. Amy Carmichael's books, especially *Edges of His Ways*, have touched me profoundly.

A missionary to India, Amy Carmichael spent the final twenty years of her life confined to her room or bed. She was disabled by illness, but she was hardly "confined." She prayed for the needs of the world. She wrote to her co-workers, staff, and children of the large orphanage she founded, sharing with them insights she gleaned from her suffering. God used her suffering to sharpen her knowledge of his character. Now, scores of years later, God is still using her insights to sharpen my view of him.

In her book *The Path of Suffering*, Elisabeth Elliot defines suffering as "Having something that you *don't* want or not having something that you *do* want." Elisabeth has modeled through her life and books that suffering is not for nothing, that God can redeem our suffering and use it to bless us and others.

The verse from 1 Peter 2 tells us that we are called to suffer. I am trying to embrace suffering as a blessed privilege. Through suffering I hope to understand more fully what Christ endured for me. Through my suffering I can identify with other people who suffer, and I can be encouraging to them through prayer.

Suffering Savior, use my suffering. Help me to consider this unwanted illness as part of your call on me today. Thank you that I can study and learn of how Jesus went before me. Thank you for biographies of others who have suffered and flourished because of you. Thank you that it is clear that I am not alone! Amen.

—*bsm*

Job's Wise Silence

 "Then Job replied to the Lord, 'I am nothing—how could I ever find the answers? I will put my hand over my mouth in silence'" (Job 40:3-4, NLT).

As I write this meditation, I am reminded that today is the anniversary of the tragic crash of TWA flight 800. That crash occurred within an hour's drive from our home, so the story has particular poignancy to the people in our area. Many of today's news accounts focus on the efforts the government made to answer the one question on everybody's mind: Why did this occur? Though someone may someday be able to provide the final, technical answer to that question, no one can provide the grieving friends and families of the victims with the spiritual answer.

The truth is there is no answer. Nothing simple and easily defined can explain the whys of suffering and sickness. Job, in the midst of his anguish and suffering, begged God for an audience so that he could plead his case, so that he could hear God answer his question: Why?

When God responded, he did it in a way that surprised Job. Instead of justifying himself, God revealed his wisdom, majesty, power, and glory. When Job saw who God is, he could not bring himself to ask the question. All Job could say was, "Surely I spoke of things I did not understand, things too wonderful for me to know" (Job 42:3, NIV).

Isaiah 55:8 tells us that God's thoughts are not our thoughts and that his ways are not our ways. Life is going to be filled with questions we cannot answer, but there is one question God wants us to answer: Will we believe even when we do not understand? The key to faith is trusting in the One who has the answers, even when he does not reveal them to us. Spend your time seeking God, being enveloped in his love, and you will be able to trust the God of love with the difficult questions of life.

Who is like you, O Lord, who is like you? As the heavens are higher than the earth, so are your ways higher than my ways. I thank you that you are such an awesome and majestic God! Amen.

 —*gf*

Seeing the Big Picture

 "God has made everything beautiful for its own time. . . . But even so, people cannot see the whole scope of God's work from beginning to end" (Ecclesiastes 3:11, NLT).

We have to admit that we spend most of our lives seeing the world from a very limited perspective. We are often bound to the present, with very little awareness of how our daily experiences are related to a larger picture. But occasionally we have times of clarity, a moment in which we see the big picture.

I recently had a moment of clarity while driving on the Oregon coast. New residents of Oregon, my husband and I were spending our first days exploring this wild, majestic coast. We were delighted by coves and cliffs, roaring breakers and spouting waves. At one point, on a mere whim, we turned off Route 101 and followed a road marked with a sign that said "auto route to Cape Perpetua Lookout." After our car labored up the steep road, we got out and followed the trail to the lookout point. When we saw what lay below us, we were speechless. It was awesomely beautiful. From the vantage point of a thousand feet up, we could see down the coast for thirty miles to the coves and cliffs we had explored earlier that day. How different they looked from up there. We could see how each curvature of the coastline fit into the others, how each was related. From the other side of the lookout, we could see for thirty miles in the other direction to the villages and coves we would visit later in the day.

As we drove down from the lookout point, I realized that God also gives us those moments of clarity about our lives, moments when he reveals to us the larger picture, a glimpse of his work in us. Have you had any moments of clarity about how your illness fits into the big picture? Has the Lord given you a glimpse of how he might use your situation in the larger scope of his work? If he has, hold on to that glimpse and let it nourish and comfort you in times of discouragement.

God of the big picture, thank you for allowing me to be part of your plan. Thank you for assuring me that you will use even my years of pain and suffering as part of your beautiful work. Amen.
        —lv

Every Purpose

"To every thing there is a season, and a time to every purpose under the heaven" (Ecclesiastes 3:1, KJV).

For twenty-nine years, I had tacitly understood that life has seasons, each with its rhythm and responsibilities. There is a time to be a student and a time to teach, a time to grow up and a time to nurture others, a time to prepare and a time to do.

I did not schedule an automobile accident. And I did not anticipate that poor health would continue to limit me thirteen years later. I had assumed that recovery would proceed, and I would be quickly back to work. I was wrong. My strength disintegrated. I lost my health and my ability to concentrate. I lost my career, and with it my financial security and private health insurance. I also lost most of my social support. Ability turned into disability and frustration.

After a half dozen years of fighting the timing of my medical retirement, I began to understand the deeper truth that God sets both the pace and the agenda. His seasons and purposes are perfect.

Every day I am reminded that what I want to do is not necessarily what I am able to do. I am frequently overwhelmed, and I strain to function at the peak of my uneven endurance and ability.

The lesson for me is clear: I must not be tempted to think that God's purposes are not being achieved during this season of illness. By his schedule, he orders the times for me to be refreshed and to be fatigued. His Spirit will lead me to full obedience in the work he has prepared in advance for me to do. His purposes will be accomplished as he has determined.

In his mercy, God reveals himself. Faithfully, he held on to me through despair and disability. He has shown me his hand in my life and my moments. I know that he holds not only all time and seasons—he also holds me.

Lord of the seasons of life, thank you for ordaining my times and my service, my circumstances and my fruit. Help me to trust you more fully when I feel out of season. Amen.

—ns

Stronger through Adversity

 "I am the true vine, and my Father is the gardener. He cuts off every branch that doesn't produce fruit, and he prunes the branches that do bear fruit so they will produce even more" (John 15:1-2, NLT).

The first time I pruned my rose bushes, I found the task strangely disturbing. It did not make sense to me to cut off perfectly healthy branches to make the plant grow stronger. But when I saw the results the following year—bigger, better, and more prolific flowers—I never again questioned the value of pruning. I got more and more skillful each time and was thankful that I did not have to convince the rose bushes that I knew what I was doing.

When Jesus compares us to the branches of the true vine in John 15, he not only reminds us that pruning is necessary for growth but also that through the painful act of pruning, God is affirming us for continued ministry. The nonfruitful branches are cut and thrown away; only the useful branches are cut back.

In a similar way, when God allows his "fruitful servants" to suffer, it is not because he wants to cause them pain but rather because he knows that through suffering they will become stronger and better than before. For some people, then, adversity and suffering are God's mark of approval, his way of saying, "I know you can handle this, and though it is hard for you right now, it will make you stronger and more useful to me in the long term."

If we focus on the short term, we will see only painful endings during the pruning process. What we must remember is that God sees the bigger picture, the beginning of a new life for us. We must remember that he loves us and that he knows what he is doing.

Father, the Master Gardener, I know that you love and value me, and I trust you with my life. Help me to remember that the adversity I am experiencing because of illness can make me a stronger, more useful person. Amen.

—*lvv*

Mercy in the Sky

"Your mercy, O Lord, is in the heavens, and Your faithfulness reaches to the clouds" (Psalm 36:5, NKJV).

I awoke this morning feeling oppressed by hopelessness. I do not normally feel hopeless. But for the past few days, I have felt a hopelessness so deep that I could not talk myself out of it or pray myself out of it or read myself out of it. Not even passages from the Bible seemed to touch the despair I was feeling. I knew in my head that the hopeful verses I found in Scripture were true; I just could not feel it in my heart.

Before I was even done with my morning shower, I was in tears. I cried through breakfast. As I prayed with my husband, I cried and could barely finish my request: "Lord, show me your presence."

After my husband left for work, I returned to the bedroom to tidy it up a bit. *Oh,* I thought, *another day of rain. That doesn't help.*

That's when I first saw it. Outside the bedroom window. It was the faintest hint of a rainbow. At first it was only the height of the neighbor's house. But as I stood at the window and watched the prismatic band, it stretched upward. Soon the rainbow was twice as big as it had been when I first saw it. Then it arched into a cloud, slowly came out the other side, and bent its way to the horizon. Within a ten-minute period, the tiny shaft had grown into a full rainbow.

It took my breath away. I was overcome with the realization that in his mercy, God had shown me his presence in that rainbow, that symbol of his unending grace. It was as if he spoke to me: "It's okay. I am with you. I *will* be with you."

God is always with us, even when we cannot see him or feel his presence. In his mercy he reminds us that his grace and love are unending. When we are discouraged, we can point to times when God has clearly shown himself to us.

Lord, your mercies *are* new every morning. Thank you for showing me your presence in sometimes surprising ways. Help me to be confident of your love for me even when I cannot see you. Especially when I cannot see you. Amen.
—*lv*

God's Presence in Pain

 "You know when I sit down or stand up. You know my every thought when far away. You chart the path ahead of me and tell me where to stop and rest. Every moment you know where I am" (Psalm 139:1-3, NLT).

Watching me struggle with relentless pain through my years with CFIDS, my husband has said with loving tenderness: "I wish I could trade bodies with you, feel your pain for you. I hate to see you suffer." Such love and compassion are indeed comforting, but the fact is, pain is a singular experience and can easily make us feel isolated and alone.

Many times pain has awakened me in the night. I quietly creep out of bed fearing that my constant tossing and turning will keep my husband awake as well. These are lonely hours. I am too sleepy to read, too muddle-headed to think straight. I have no one to talk to. My body becomes a lonely prison, an isolated crucible of suffering.

But instead of despairing during these sleepless nights, I find comfort by thinking of another who loves me deeply—One who knows every sensation my body is feeling, every stabbing pain, every burning joint, every inch of my exploding head. He is the One who knit me together in my mother's womb. He knows when I sit and when I rise. He knows when I hurt and when I am afraid.

Psalm 139 reveals the physical intimacy God has with us. He knew us before we were conceived. He knows when we exhale and blink.

How wonderful it is that through the gift of salvation we can have a personal, intimate relationship with God—a comforter who knows us through and through, a friend who is always near, who never slumbers or sleeps, a God who suffered and died for our sins so that we would not be alone in our pain.

All-knowing Father, you are aware of everything I experience. Thank you for knowing and loving me so intimately. Thank you for holding me in your arms when I struggle with physical pain. Your love sustains me and delivers me from my despair. Amen.

—lvv

Real Treasure

 "Don't store up treasures here on earth, where they can be eaten by moths and get rusty, and where thieves break in and steal. Store your treasures in heaven, where they will never become moth-eaten or rusty and where they will be safe from thieves. Wherever your treasure is, there your heart and thoughts will also be" (Matthew 6:19-21, NLT).

I do not have the strength or energy to work and earn money. As a result I have been unable to provide my wife with some of the material things that my friends and acquaintances have. And I will admit that at times this has really bothered me.

But then the Lord reminds me of two very important truths. The first is that what we consider to be wealth in this world is common and ordinary to him, lacking any true and eternal value. Second, true wealth is found not in things on earth but in knowing him. I have had designer suits eaten by moths, fancy sunglasses lost overboard, money stolen, collectible treasures found to be fakes, and valuable antiques ruined by water. But I have never had the Lord abandon me.

Even though exhaustion has robbed me of my ability to work, it has not robbed me of the opportunity to know God better. In fact, through our illnesses, my wife and I have come to know the Lord in profound and startlingly real ways. We have seen his faithfulness as he sustained us through very difficult years. We have seen his compassion as he has brought friends and family members to help us. We have seen his redeeming power as he has taken our broken bodies and used them to "feed" other people spiritually. What treasures! We are rich people, indeed.

Lord, thank you for giving me true wealth, a glimpse of who you are. Help me not to set my heart on earthly treasures, which are here today but gone tomorrow. Please help me to want true wealth, the things that matter to you. Amen.

—gf

Looking beyond What We Can See

 "Therefore we do not lose heart. Though outwardly we are wasting away, yet inwardly we are being renewed day by day. For our light and momentary troubles are achieving for us an eternal glory that far outweighs them all. So we fix our eyes not on what is seen, but on what is unseen. For what is seen is temporary, but what is unseen is eternal" (2 Corinthians 4:16-18, NIV).

Some days I feel as if I am wasting away. The sickness that rages in my body has robbed me of many things—my health, my ability to serve God actively, my energy to spend with family members and friends. Day by day the "momentary troubles" of illness and fatigue can be overwhelming. Sometimes I am afraid I will lose heart.

But if our focus is today's—or tomorrow's—pain and discomfort, the picture we are drawing of ourselves is rough and incomplete. We are much more than the sum total of our illness or the symptoms it brings.

In his book *Dawn without Darkness*, Anthony Padovano writes:

"The boundaries of life and the limits of hope cannot be drawn with the crayons of times and space." We must look beyond what we see and refocus our attention on the unseen. God desires to help us look through the pain, which is temporary, and focus on our relationship to him, which is eternal.

If we are able to see with God's eyes, we can grasp that this temporary physical illness is not just a distraction; it is a vital part of the renovation of our souls. Through it God renews us every day. Increasingly, we will be able to look beyond the glare, feel beyond the pain, and listen beyond the furor to perceive what God is doing in and through this illness. No matter how overwhelming today's pain may be, when we catch a glimpse of this renewing activity, we will be able to "take heart."

Dear Lord, I want the picture of my life to reflect what you are doing in the eternal chambers of my soul. Please give me the ability and the courage to look beyond the pain and focus on the life and hope of your eternal glory. Amen.

  —ph

Confidently Waiting

 "As for me, I look to the Lord for his help. I wait confidently for God to save me, and my God will certainly hear me" (Micah 7:7, NLT).

I don't know about you, but I hate waiting. I don't like waiting for a holiday to come. I don't like waiting in line. I just don't like waiting.

But since I have been ill, I find that waiting is all I do! I wait for my strength to return. I wait for "normal" life to come back. I wait for medical science to find a treatment for the illness that has hijacked my body. And I resist that waiting.

This verse from the Old Testament prophesy of Micah instructs us to wait confidently for God. In this context waiting is a good thing. It is a desirable action.

The word *wait* is found in one of my Bibles 101 times. Many of those uses refer to waiting for God. What does that mean? To wait for God means to earnestly expect and hope that he will act on our behalf, that he will hear us and save us.

What are the rewards of waiting confidently for God? A passage in Isaiah tells us, "But those who wait on the Lord will find new strength. . . . They will run and not grow weary" (Isa. 40:31, NLT). We will find new strength because the burden of our illness is transferred off our shoulders onto God's. It now is in his hands to restore our strength at the time that he knows is best for us. It is his responsibility to take care of all of our needs—physical, mental, emotional, spiritual, and financial. By waiting confidently on God, I allow him to control my life. I can cease my struggling, rest, and wait patiently for him to do what needs to be done.

Dear God, waiting is one of the hardest things for me to do. I like to be in control of my life. Help me to trust you fully and to wait confidently for you. Amen.

  —cf

Why Am I Hidden?

 "In the shadow of his hand he hid me; he made me into a polished arrow and concealed me in his quiver. He said to me, 'You are my servant, Israel, in whom I will display my splendor.' But I said, 'I have labored to no purpose; I have spent my strength in vain and for nothing. Yet what is due me is in the Lord's hand, and my reward is with my God'" (Isaiah 49:2-4, NIV).

I have spent most of my teenage years and the first few years of adulthood living with CFIDS. I haven't been in school much during this time. When I was able to attend classes with my peers, I still felt the hardness and loneliness caused by this sickness. I remember a particular instance of looking out my window on a weekend night and seeing my friends go out. I was not part of the scene. I had to rest.

Suffering serves to intensify isolation and the feeling of aloneness. I found myself asking lots of questions: Is there meaning in the midst of this less productive time? How can God use my illness? What is the purpose of my life if I am stuck at home, unable to adequately maintain relationships?

These verses from Isaiah 49 have helped me to find some answers to those questions. It is God himself who has set me aside and "hidden" me. Through this suffering he has polished me and concealed me in his quiver. The arrow goes unused not because it is not ready. He has placed it—ready for action—in his quiver so that he can use it at any point.

I came to realize that my value is not in what I could or could not do. My reward is in the Lord's hand. What a release! The reward doesn't depend on me and my ability or disability but lies with the One who made me as I am and continues to sharpen me. The Lord knows my value. He knows me intimately. He called me before my birth (Isa. 49:1). I can trust him with my future.

Father, give me rest in your quiver. Thank you that you have not abandoned me and that you will not neglect me. I give myself wholly over to you because you have the reward that my heart longs for. Amen.

—nm

What Am I Worth?

 "But now, thus says the Lord, your creator, O Jacob, and he who formed you, O Israel, 'Do not fear, for I have redeemed you; I have called you by name; you are Mine! When you pass through the waters, I will be with you; and through the rivers, they will not overflow you. When you walk through the fire, you will not be scorched, nor will the flame burn you. . . . You are precious in My sight, . . . you are honored and I love you'" (Isaiah 43:1-4, NASB).

Society today puts a great deal of emphasis on self-worth. It tells us that if we were not born with a great self-image (or if we have lost it), we can earn it, buy it, borrow it. We can find self-worth in a book, a bottle, or a video. Mostly, though, we try to secure self-worth through possessions, power, performance, or other people.

What happens when these external props are taken away from us through an accident, illness, or other unexpected circumstances? What's left? Many people would tell us that nothing is left. We are reduced to nobody.

God, the Creator who formed you in your mother's womb, disagrees! What we do or have does not define our worth. We are valuable simply because God says we are. Look what God says to us.

> You are redeemed—That is your value.
> You are mine—That is your security.
> You are precious—That is your worth.
> You are honored—That is your significance.
> You are loved—That is your assurance.

No job or Christian service could offer all that to us. The possessions we accumulate on this earth will one day burn away. People will fail and disappoint us, but God's love for us never changes or disappoints. Even if we are sick, poor, tired, or unproductive, his love for us is absolute, unconditional, and never-ending. Now that does a lot for our sense of self-worth!

Gracious Lord, even in my pain and weakness, I am still precious to you. Thank you for loving me enough to redeem me with your own life. I love you and honor you. Amen.

—rr

Staying by the Stuff

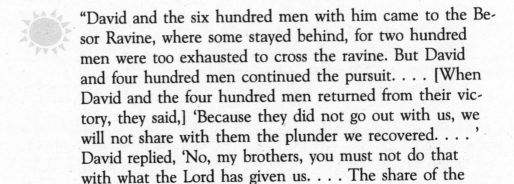

"David and the six hundred men with him came to the Besor Ravine, where some stayed behind, for two hundred men were too exhausted to cross the ravine. But David and four hundred men continued the pursuit. . . . [When David and the four hundred men returned from their victory, they said,] 'Because they did not go out with us, we will not share with them the plunder we recovered. . . .' David replied, 'No, my brothers, you must not do that with what the Lord has given us. . . . The share of the man who stayed with the supplies is to be the same as that of him who went down to the battle'" (1 Samuel 30:9-10, 22-24, NIV).

In the middle of a battle, some of David's men were too tired to go on. David instructed them to stay and guard the supplies. Later, when the victorious troops returned to camp, the returning men did not want to share the spoils of war with the men who had "stayed with the stuff." David's response was that God had given them the victory and because of that, all the men would share equally in the reward.

Of course, I identify with those who stayed behind, too exhausted to go on. It is hard being the one who is left at home to rest when others are active and out meeting the challenges of life. It is hard to remember my identity as a soldier or a provider or a parent when I am too tired to do my job.

The spiritual principle revealed in these verses, though, is that God's efforts win the battle, not ours. And when he gives the victory, *both* kinds of soldiers share in the reward. We forget that God is at work in our children and families, drawing them to himself and maturing them. We think it all is because we are such great parents and we are doing so many things right. Then, when we cannot do the job as we planned, we have to realize *again* that it is God who gives the victory. We are reminded that both the exhausted parent who is faithful to support those in the battle and the parent who is on the front line share the rewards of the struggle.

Gracious God, thank you that you are just as concerned with those of us who "stay with the stuff" as you are with those who seem to be in the thick of activity. Help me to remember that as I stay behind, I can pray for my family and save some energy to welcome them home when they are weary. Amen.

—*hg*

Using an Empty Jar

"There are different kinds of gifts, but the same Spirit. There are different kinds of service, but the same Lord. There are different kinds of working, but the same God works all of them in all" (1 Corinthians 12:4-6, NIV).

When life situations drain us of energy, we are tempted to feel empty, devoid of any ability to serve others. But we need to remember that our debilitation need not hinder our service to God. Even if we are very limited compared to what we were able to do before, God can use us.

We may not be able to get out of bed or attend fellowship events, but we can build the church. We can still enter into God's presence and engage him in prayer. When a friend needs to talk, we can listen and counsel. By marking our calendars to remember friends' special dates such as birthdays, anniversaries, work deadlines, or travel plans, we can supplement prayer with direct encouragement through notes, electronic mail, or phone messages. When someone becomes tempted or discouraged, we may be the only ones available to discern and support.

Our responsibility for service is not contingent on good health, although the expression of service may be influenced by our condition. Obviously if we are too weak to cook dinner for ourselves, we won't be able to do physical work for someone else. But we can do other things. When we are too feeble even to verbalize, we can enter into God's presence without words.

Gifts, service, and working all require people to do and to receive. Although we are weakened by fatigue, we are perfectly placed in the body of Christ to support and encourage one another as he has called us to do.

In our frailty, God uses our gifts and manifests his strength. Physical illness cannot separate us from his love or prevent our service.

Dear Lord, thank you for giving the members of your body different kinds of gifts. Thank you for the valuable treasures you have hidden within our seemingly empty vessels. Help me to use my gifts even in my affliction to draw your body closer. Amen.

—ns

Illness Gives Us Empathy

"He comforts us every time we have trouble, so that we can comfort others when they have trouble. We can comfort them with the same comfort that God gives us"
(2 Corinthians 1:4, TEB).

When we are afflicted with a chronic illness, we often turn inward, focusing on our own immediate suffering and problems. We may stumble through each day in a haze, putting all of our effort on our immediate survival. We may lose sight of others around us. We want them to hear our suffering, our losses, but in our focus on ourselves we fail to listen to them.

I often look back on how little I understood about individual losses before I became ill. I had never experienced great loss in any area of my life, and I certainly did not expect it in the near future. I was coasting along, anaesthetized to the suffering that was all around me. My perception of a great loss was a low score on a test or a mild disagreement with a friend. While I may have had a certain amount of sympathy for the problems of those around me, I surely did not have empathy.

What a difference my illness has made in my perception! I now have experienced many losses in many areas of my life. I can no longer listen to people's suffering with the detachment I had before. I know how it feels, and my heart is moved. My own suffering can be a source of wisdom and strength for others to draw on if I let it.

Our illness can often give us another commodity that those around us may not have—time. While many people who are healthy may be too busy to see the need and suffering of others, our lives are slower, and we are aware of what is around us. We may not have the energy to do many things, but we can listen, send cards, and encourage those in need.

If you have suffered a great deal, draw on the reservoir of strength and wisdom your suffering has created. Spend some time showing empathy and understanding to someone in need around you.

Dear God, help cause my hardships to be a source of strength and understanding to people who are facing difficulties. Help me to listen to their struggles and enable me to comfort them with the comfort you have given me. Amen.

—*cm*

Just As I Am

"'I tell you the truth,' he said, 'this poor widow has put in more than all the others. All these people gave their gifts out of their wealth; but she out of her poverty put in all she had to live on'" (Luke 21:3-4, NIV).

Charlotte Elliott, who lived from 1789 to 1871, suffered from an unspecified illness that caused fatigue, weakness, and pain. Her condition kept her housebound for much of her adult life. During this time, she wrote hundreds of hymns, one of which is the beautiful and well known, "Just As I Am."

This hymn has always made me cry as I realize that God loves and accepts me just as I am, despite my sinfulness. But after hearing of Charlotte Elliott's chronic illness and disability, the song took on a larger meaning: God can use us, if we are willing, just as we are—poor, wretched, blind, sick, or fatigued. Our limited capacity does not matter to him. What matters is our faithfulness, our willingness to give ourselves to him.

These thoughts shed new light for me on God's view of giving. I thought of the story of the widow's offering in Luke. Jesus looked up and saw a poor widow putting in two coins, giving literally all she had.

Today, as in Jesus' day, the world leads us to believe that more is better, that fulfillment is based on how much we achieve, how much we give. When illness tears us away from our livelihood, from our ministry, the results can destroy our souls. Anything we have to offer seems insignificant compared to what we used to be able to do. What we must remember is that God sees things differently. As Jesus points out, he values our willingness to give, not how much we give.

Father, I confess that I have often believed that more is better. Teach me in all humility to give what I can and be satisfied, knowing that I have pleased you. Thank you for loving me, accepting me, and drawing me to yourself—just as I am. Amen.
— *lvv*

Do I Have Significance?

 "And all of us [Christians] have had that veil removed so that we can be mirrors that brightly reflect the glory of the Lord. And as the Spirit of the Lord works within us, we become more and more like him and reflect his glory even more" (2 Corinthians 3:18, NLT).

While walking in my garden one day, I spotted a lone flower growing between two rocks. "Only God could have planted that flower there," I exclaimed. Perhaps I identified with this flower, there alone, between the rocks, in the shade. If the flower could have spoken, I wonder if it would have revealed feelings of insignificance compared with the other flowers blooming a few feet away in the sun?

This lone flower seemed more beautiful to me than the others because it was blooming in the middle of rocks, in the middle of hard circumstances. Yet, this flower was doing what it was created to do: draw attention to its Creator. This was God's purpose for his entire creation from the beginning. But after sin entered the world, human beings no longer felt it was important to draw attention to their Creator.

Instead, we wanted to draw attention only to ourselves. We still spend so much of our energy searching for success and significance.

For the chronically fatigued, this burden for personal significance is unbearable. But we do not need to carry it. We are in a shady, rocky area, so to speak. It is hard to see others thriving in the sun. But we are no less significant than those blessed with health. As we become more God-conscious and less self-conscious, an intimacy with God develops, resulting in a restful yielding to him and his will for our lives. God can use us just the way we are without our *doing* a single thing in order to turn others' attention to himself. Now can you think of anything more significant than that?

We may feel as if we are "between a rock and a hard place." Yet actually we are in the best place we could be because God planted us here. Just as that one lone flower drew my attention to God, we, too, can mirror his glory.

Lord, when that cry for significance surfaces, help me to turn my attention from myself to you. I want to be a mirror, Lord, so that others may see your beauty more and more reflected in me. Amen.

  —*mm*

God's Expectations of Us

 "If you are really eager to give, it isn't important how much you are able to give. God wants you to give what you have, not what you don't have" (2 Corinthians 8:12, NLT).

Many people who suffer from chronic illness feel that they have very little to give to others. Physical strength, stamina, financial resources, mental acuity—all these were the wells from which we had previously drawn to give to God and others. Now, those wells are dry.

Relationships have changed. We, who once were the givers, have become the receivers. We are the needy ones. Many people do not understand this change. Many friendships do not withstand the transition.

Expectations have also changed. Before illness and fatigue struck, many of us were competent people on whom others relied. Now we are unable to meet those expectations.

While we may not be able to fulfill other people's expectations of us, it is comforting to know that God's expectations of us are realistic. He measures our giving not in overall quantities but in relation to the amount we have to give. He is pleased with a heart that is willing to give. Though the amount of the gift may be small, he judges its worth by the size of the storehouse from which it is given.

We may often feel that what we do have to give is overlooked or not appreciated. When we are struggling every day with the effects of a debilitating illness, it costs us much more to give much less. It may be all we can do to be cheerful in an attempt to encourage those around us and to shield them from our suffering. Isn't it refreshing to know that God appreciates our gifts, no matter how small they are? He sees the *true* value of each one.

Dear God, help me to concentrate on your expectations rather than the expectations of others. Help me to give to you out of what I have rather than try to give to you what I don't have. Amen.

—*cm*

With All My Strength

 "Love the Lord your God with all your heart and with all your soul and with all your mind and with all your strength" (Mark 12:30, NIV).

This verse from Mark 12 was a centerpiece of my life even before my illness. I always wanted to love God with *all* my heart, soul, mind, and strength. But I have never felt as if I have been able to do that.

Once I became sick, I was even less able. I was almost totally bedridden for the first six years of my illness. I had so little strength that I could not go to church. My brain could not process words, so I could not read my Bible anymore. And my concentration was so damaged that I could not pray, other than desperate pleas for mercy and deliverance. All of this debilitation led to an overwhelming sense that I had failed in the only thing that truly mattered.

Or had I?

After many years of grieving because I *longed* to pray but couldn't, God began to show me that as long as I still *desired* to commune with him, I did love him. He showed me that although I had almost no strength to love him in the way that healthy people can love him, I did love him with all my strength.

What a comfort that can be to us! God does not require us to have a lot of strength; he just requires that we love him with whatever strength we have. Even if you, too, are unable to maintain the normal spiritual disciplines of reading the Bible, worshiping with other believers, or praying as you did before you were debilitated, you can love God with all your heart and soul and mind and strength.

O God, thank you for your mercy and grace. Thank you that even during the times when I feel cut off from you, nothing, not even this horrible illness, can truly separate me from you. I do love you, Lord, and I desire to love you with all my heart, soul, mind, and strength. Amen.

—sf

The Right Measuring Stick

 "We do not dare to classify or compare ourselves with some who commend themselves. When they measure themselves by themselves and compare themselves with themselves, they are not wise. We, however, will not boast beyond proper limits, but will confine our boasting to the field God has assigned to us" (2 Corinthians 10:12-13, NIV).

I am most dissatisfied with my life and limitations when I begin comparing myself to others. Today's media bombard me with enticing images of what I should be. If I succumb to television or magazines, I'm confronted with bodies that have been pushed, pulled, tucked, and retouched into amazing pictures of youth and beauty. I look at myself and see a pale, wrinkled, flabby, diseased body. I feel depressed.

At church I see others serving God in ways I no longer am able. Why does God enable her to sing with such strength? Why is he able to play the piano so well? Why has she been blessed with the energy to care for her family and teach a Bible study as well? All I can do on a "good day" is wash my hair, take a rest, do some laundry, take another rest, cook dinner, take a rest—and the day is over. I feel worthless.

When we compare ourselves to other people, we are placing ourselves outside the circle God has placed us in. When that happens, we can become bitter, jealous, and dissatisfied. We need to realize that we are using the wrong measuring stick. We need to remember that our only standard of comparison should be Christ and his Word. What we look like and what we do are not nearly as important as who we are.

Even on a "bad day" we can be loving. When we can't work, we can be encouraging. When we can't serve on a committee, we can be faithful in prayer. When we can't be physically active, we can delight in God's will. Even within the limitations of our fatigue, we can be men and women who trust God's Word.

Lord, forgive me for comparing myself to other people. Help me to remember to use the right measuring stick: you and your Word. Amen.

—rr

The Worth of Suffering

"For our struggle is not against flesh and blood, but against the rulers, against the authorities, against the powers of this dark world and against the spiritual forces of evil in the heavenly realms" (Ephesians 6:12, NIV).

I have often pondered why God would allow unspeakable suffering. I have never found a satisfactory explanation. I have always felt that God does have a reason and purpose for suffering, and that makes it easier to bear. But, to be honest, I don't understand what that reason is.

Some people have said that my suffering will allow me to help others in similar circumstances. However, for years I did not have enough strength to have contact with other people, let alone to minister to those with similar problems. Others have said that God uses illness to develop character, and yet my character, in fact my whole personality, mind, and emotions, have seemed as poisoned and disabled as my physical body.

While I do believe that God uses suffering in many ways, including helping others and building character, these seemed to be horribly weak reasons for what I was enduring. I did, however, find great comfort in the book of Job and was thankful that God revealed the spiritual battle that took place over Job. Without Job's knowledge, God allowed Satan to attack him. Job's ability to love and worship God even in the midst of horrible suffering won a battle in the spiritual realm.

I have often wondered whether a battle is being waged over me in the spiritual realm. Ephesians 6:12 tells us that our battle is against spiritual forces of evil in the heavenly realms. This possibility has given purpose to my suffering. Even when I had not recovered enough to get out of bed, my simple love for God was a testimony against all the demons and powers of darkness. Even when I didn't see any victory in my body, there was victory in the spiritual realm.

Heavenly Father, thank you that you do have purposes for my suffering even if I don't understand them fully. Thank you for showing me that all of this experience is part of a spiritual battle and that you are glorified by my faithfulness to you. Help me, O God, to overcome all the power of the enemy. Amen.

—sf

Lord, I Want to Serve

"Be still, and know that I am God;
  I will be exalted among the nations,
I will be exalted in the earth" (Psalm 46:10, NIV).

"But Lord, I want to serve you." In the years that I have been debilitated by illness and fatigue, I have prayed this prayer often. Each time I voice this request, the Lord answers, "My child, I don't want or need your service. I can get my work done with or without you. What I want from you is your love and trust. Just be still."

My desire to serve the Lord sounds so spiritual and unselfish, right? I say I want to serve God by serving others. But maybe my desire to serve is really a selfish desire. I am embarrassed to say that maybe I really want to do things for others so that I don't have to accept their service to me. Maybe I am seeking to gratify myself by being the benefactor because in some way that makes me superior. I don't like the feeling of being inferior, of needing to have others do for me. I don't like to admit my own weakness.

But God wants me to realize my total dependency on him. He

wants me to understand that all I can ever give to him (or anyone else) is what he has first given me. He doesn't need my money; he owns the cattle on a thousand hills (Ps. 50:10). He doesn't need my nursing care; he can heal with a word (John 4:43-54). He doesn't need my transportation; he moved Philip instantaneously (Acts 8:28-40). He doesn't need my meal preparation; he fed crowds of thousands with five loaves and two small fish (Mark 6:30-44). He doesn't need anything from you or me.

But the stupendous truth is that the all-powerful Creator and Sustainer of the universe wants our love and trust. He wants *us*. He doesn't *need* us; he is complete in himself. But he chooses to desire our affection and attention.

Father, forgive me for my stubborn pride that thinks I have to give you something in order to have value. Thank you for reminding me that what you really want from me is my love and trust. Help me to be still and know—truly know—that you are God. Amen.

    —jeh

Why Did You Make Me Like This?

 "But who are you, O man, to talk back to God? 'Shall what is formed say to him who formed it, "Why did you make me like this?"' Does not the potter have the right to make out of the same lump of clay some pottery for noble purposes and some for common use?" (Romans 9:20-21, NIV).

"Mommy, no. Not again. *Please* don't let the doctor do it again." The young boy pleaded with his mother not to have the doctor give him yet another spinal tap. Although the mother's heart was breaking when she heard her son's cries, she gave consent to have the painful procedure done on her leukemic child. Did she explain why this pain was being inflicted? No, her son was too young to understand. Did she love him? With all of her heart!

Do you ever feel as this boy did? Do you wonder why God is letting us hurt, why he made us like this? Do you want to pummel on God's chest and ask for an explanation?

Like the mother, God doesn't always explain his purposes to us because we are often incapable of understanding. But does he love us? With all of his heart!

Instead of answering our questions, God gives us comfort. "Be still, and know that I am God" (Ps. 46:10, NIV). These words redirect our attention from who we are to who God is. Scripture reveals him to be the sovereign One, who has absolute authority over his created universe and everyone in it. He is the God of *power*, who spoke and the raging waves obeyed his voice. He is the God of *compassion*, who touched blind eyes and made them see, who wiped away his own tears and brought back life to a dead man's body. *This* is the God who made us. *This* is the God who loves us.

God is the potter; we are the clay. We can rebel and become hardened and bitter, or we can submit to him and become more like Jesus. The molding is like the child's treatment, not meant to harm us but to make us better. What better place could there be than in the loving, sovereign hands of our Maker?

All-knowing Potter, help me to trust you with all of my whys and whens and why nots. May my confidence in who you are overcome my questions about why you made me like this. Amen.

—*mm*

Forgive Them?

"But when you are praying, first forgive anyone you are holding a grudge against, so that your Father in heaven will forgive your sins, too" (Mark 11:25, NLT).

Several times during the years I have been ill, people have hurt me. I don't think that they necessarily intended the hurt, but their judgmental attitudes or flippant comments or unwillingness to understand have caused me pain. Gradually I have come to realize that I must forgive them for their thoughtlessness and insensitivity.

Forgiveness is not a one-time act. If a person has deeply hurt and wounded me, I sometimes find that when I hear that person's name, the hurt feelings resurface very quickly. If I do not remind myself that I have already prayed and forgiven that person, I will begin to dwell on my hurt feelings and open the door to bitterness. Bitterness does not hurt the one who hurt me. Bitterness can, however, destroy me.

Forgiveness is an ongoing process until the matter is settled and I am able to fully forgive and love the one who has wounded me. In his booklet *Freedom through Forgiveness*, Ted Haggard says,

As you are praying, verbally express to the Lord your forgiveness every day. As you do this over a period of time, God's grace will break through that tough exterior produced by hurt and grant genuine forgiveness in your heart. *Force yourself to forgive.* Don't wait for it to happen naturally. It won't happen. You must take control in the name of Jesus. Each time you do this, God will honor your obedience and fill your heart with forgiveness. Greater freedom in your prayer life will result, and the Lord will greatly develop your spiritual potential.

When we feel bitterness arising because of how people have treated us, we can choose to forgive the person rather than nurse our hurts.

Dear God, thank you for repeatedly forgiving me for the times I have hurt you and others. I confess that I am weak and don't want to forgive. Help me to have the strength and courage to continue forgiving those who have hurt me until the forgiveness is genuine and I can love them. Amen.
    —cf

Why This Waste?

 "Now when Jesus was in Bethany, at the home of Simon the leper, a woman came to Him with an alabaster vial of very costly perfume, and she poured it upon His head as He reclined at the table. But the disciples were indignant when they saw this, and said, 'Why this waste?'" (Matthew 26:6-8, NASB).

"Couldn't this perfume have been sold and the money given to the poor?" demanded a self-righteous disciple.

"Yeah," another joined in, "a whole year's salary wasted on Jesus' feet!"

But Jesus rebuked the disciples, "Leave Mary alone. She has done a good thing. She has done what she could."

When I look at my weakened body, I ask the same kinds of questions the disciples asked. Couldn't I be using my degree to teach in a mission school? Couldn't I be using my music to bless others? My education, my experience, my past—it's all a waste now!

God rebukes me, though, and says, "Your life is not a waste. I expect you to give only what you have, to do only what you can."

Have you ever considered giving your body, broken and weakened, as a living sacrifice to God? In his letter to the church in Rome, the apostle Paul says, "And so, dear brothers and sisters, I plead with you to give your bodies to God. Let them be a living and holy sacrifice" (Rom. 12:1, NLT). This command isn't just for missionaries or other full-time Christian workers. It's for all of us, even for those of us with sick and broken bodies. Like the woman who poured the perfume on Jesus' feet, you can place your body with all its sickness, pain, and fear at his feet. What you have given up as a result of illness is your sweet-smelling sacrifice to God. Your sacrifices are never wasted on him.

Lord, forgive me for thinking that my life is a waste. I give you my body, weak and broken though it is, as a living sacrifice. Accept it and use it as you choose. I trust that you are good. Amen.

—rr

What Did I Do to Deserve This?

 "And I am sure that God, who began the good work within you, will continue his work until it is finally finished on that day when Christ Jesus comes back again" (Philippians 1:6, NLT).

I just finished talking to a friend whose niece is suffering from CFIDS and other fatiguing illnesses. The niece, who is the mother of two sick children, is distraught. My friend asked, "What do I say to my niece when she keeps asking what she has done to deserve this illness?"

Have you ever asked that question? I have. More than once. I would like to know what I did wrong so that I can undo it! But inherent in that wish is the underlying assumption that we somehow control our lives. That, however, is not true. God is in control of my life, and if he has allowed a disabling illness to touch me at this point, then I can trust that he knows what he's doing.

I told my friend to tell her niece this: "You didn't do anything to deserve this! It's not what *you* did; it's what God is trying to do. He has begun a good work in you, and he will continue until that work is done." That is the scriptural truth. We don't always know why things happen. In fact, we rarely know. So, although it's normal to agonize, cry out, weep, and complain, we must ultimately trust ourselves to God's good purposes. He has started a good work in our lives, and we must trust that he will finish it, even if he chooses to use illness as one of his tools in the process!

Father, help me to see that my illness and debilitation are not some sort of punishment for something we did. I take comfort in knowing not only that you are working in my life but also that you will continue to work in me until the job is done, until I am the way you want me to be. Help me to trust your goodness and rely on your wisdom. Amen.

—bsm

How Can This Experience Be Good?

 "And we know that God causes everything to work together for the good of those who love God and are called according to his purpose for them" (Romans 8:28, NLT).

When we hear this verse quoted, we often think that the "good" for us is recovery from our fatiguing illness. What isn't good about that?

But while physical health seems good to us, it is not necessarily the good that God has ordained. God's good will is accomplished even though it sometimes seems to be illogical or unfair at the time. The good is what God deems to be good. We must yield to his judgment and perspective.

God does not guarantee us comfort or easy living. A comfortable life is not a measure of blessings from God, even though our culture would like us to believe that it is. God does not guarantee us relief from desperate circumstances. We cannot command God to reunite the family, restore our health, return the prodigal, or repair our relationships simply because these outcomes seem good to us. It is not wrong to desire healing friendships, peaceful family relationships, a comfortable home, excellent health, or financial security, but we must not want these things more than we want to submit to God's good purposes.

Each of our desires must be surrendered to our Lord, who will, as he has promised, cause all things to work together for our good—not for our pleasure but for our good. He will work things out for our spiritual maturity, for strengthening his body, for building his church, and for preparing us for eternity.

The question in our hearts should not be "What do I need now?" or "How can I fix this mess?" but "How can I live to the glory of God now and forever?" We can trust our lives to his good plan.

Gracious Father, you alone know what is good. Show me how to surrender my desires to you, and make me a willing participant in your divine plan. Amen.
    —ns

All of Life's Answers Questioned

 "We are hard pressed on every side, but not crushed; perplexed, but not in despair; persecuted, but not abandoned; struck down, but not destroyed" (2 Corinthians 4:8-9, NIV).

I read recently that when frogs are exposed to boiling water, they instinctively leap out of danger. But when frogs are placed in cold water that is slowly heated to the boiling point, they remain in the water until they die. Despair is like that. Most any of us would be able to recognize and resist its sudden onset, but when despair is the subtle result of years of discouragement, it can drain the very life out of us.

If you struggle with despair, I encourage you to do two things. First, seek the help of other Christians for prayer and counsel because you will not be able to combat despair alone. Second, while despair is powerful, fight back by taking every thought captive and making it obedient to Christ (2 Cor. 10:5). Fortunately, thoughts, like muscles, can be trained and fortified. People who have had strokes often have the arduous task of retraining themselves to think and act in order to function.

The antidote to despair is no different.

Start the retraining by asking yourself two very foundational questions about God's character: Is God good? (Ps. 73:1; John 10:14) and Will everything he does in your life work for a good purpose? (Rom. 8:28). If you can come to the place where you can answer yes to those two questions, those truths will act like a lifeline when despair threatens to overwhelm you.

Notice that I am not asking you if everything you are going through makes sense or if you have all the answers to why you are suffering. Surgery is never a pleasant experience, but if I believe that the physician is cutting me open for my benefit rather than my detriment, I will not despair from the surgery. It is the same with my faith in God. If I believe that what I am going through is for my spiritual benefit, I may not like it, but I won't be filled with despair.

Lord, hear my cries for help, for I am weary and discouraged. I need your strength to help me believe in your goodness and love. Amen.

—gf

Receiving a Gift We Didn't Want

 "Mary responded, 'I am the Lord's servant, and I am willing to accept whatever he wants. May everything you have said come true'" (Luke 1:38, NLT).

At some point in our lives, most of us have received a gift we didn't want. Maybe it was at Christmas, when you had your heart set on getting that soft blue sweater, but you got a snow shovel instead. You felt understandably disappointed, and you didn't know what to say.

For many of us, the situation that has drained us of energy and has left us debilitated by fatigue is a gift we never wanted. In fact, for many of us, we wonder if it is a gift at all. How do we respond to such a gift? What do we say?

Mary, the mother of Jesus, knew what it was like to get a gift she didn't want. You know the story. The angel comes to the young girl to announce: "God has decided to bless you. You will become pregnant . . ." At that point, I can imagine that Mary was no longer paying full attention to what the angel was saying. *Pregnant! How could that be? How could that be a blessing?*

While that may be what Mary thought, it isn't what she said. In response to a gift she didn't want, Mary offered one of the most profound statements of surrender: "I am the Lord's servant, and I am willing to accept whatever he wants." Mary knew who she was, and she knew who God is.

May that be true of us as well. As we fumble for a response to receiving a fatiguing condition—a gift we didn't want—may we have the confidence to know that we are the Lord's servants, for whatever that means. Then may we have the courage and faith to submit our weakened, sick bodies to the God who loves us, who is capable of turning bad things into good. May we be willing to accept whatever he chooses to do in us.

Lord, I surrender my broken life to you. I know that you love me. I am willing to accept whatever you want. Amen.
　　　—lv

Why Doesn't God Do Something?

 "'My thoughts are completely different from yours,' says the Lord. 'And my ways are far beyond anything you could imagine'" (Isaiah 55:8, NLT).

Have you ever noticed that God seldom seems to do things the way we would do them? For example, my parents gave my wife and me a whale-watching trip as an anniversary present. We rested for days, garnering all our strength in eager anticipation of witnessing one of God's most magnificent creations. But when we were on the whale-watching boat, we spent three hours looking at absolutely nothing—not a whale, not a fish, not even a bird. Nothing! Every trip that day before and after ours sighted whales, but for some reason we came back without having seen any.

I prayed fervently all the while we were on the boat, wondering why God wasn't answering such a meager request. After all, what was the big deal? In situations in which God doesn't perform the way I expect him to, I ask one simple question: Do I trust in his divine plan and wisdom for my life?

A few years ago I was at an intersection, trying to make a left-hand turn against traffic. I was already late for a doctor's appointment, so I was even more impatient as I waited for the traffic to clear. I found myself angry with God, thinking, *Would it really have been such a big deal to space the cars a little farther apart so I could make the turn and get to the appointment?* Well, as it turns out, it was a big deal. After I made my turn, I saw a car speed through a red light at the next intersection ahead of me. At that moment I realized that I would have been hit if I hadn't been delayed from making that turn.

Unfortunately, we don't often have such obvious and powerful answers to our questions about why God works the way he does. But when he does choose to reveal his goodness to us unmistakably, as he did to me that day, we are reminded to trust him even when we can't see his activity and when we don't understand his ways.

Lord, your ways definitely are beyond my understanding. But I will trust in you even when I don't understand, even when I am disappointed with how things turn out. Amen.

—*gf*

Can Any Good Come from This Illness?

 "Now to him who is able to do immeasurably more than all we ask or imagine, according to his power that is at work in us . . ." (Ephesians 3:20, NIV).

Drip, drip, drip. The IV solution flowed into my sick body three days a week for three years. As I lay on sterile white sheets and listened to hospital sounds and the moans of patients, I fought tears of depression and wondered if any good could result from this seemingly bleak trial.

As I lay there, I thought about the words from Ephesians 3:20. *Now unto him.* Yes, it was God who placed me there in that bed. When I acknowledged that, it was as if someone lifted a shade and bright sunlight streamed into my heart. The fear, dread, and depression that had been my companions when I entered the hospital doors were replaced by joy and anticipation for whatever God had in store for me!

Who is able to do immeasurably more than all we ask or imagine. My perspective changed. I was not only a patient in a hospital, but I realized that because I was there by divine appointment, I was also an ambassador representing Christ. The hospital became a kind of mission field! Patients, nurses, and staff members began coming to talk with me, and before long I was able to share what God had done and was doing in my life. These relationships continued long after my discharge from my treatments.

According to his power that is at work in us. God's love was so powerful that it reached out to these needy ones through my sick body. Some of the people who came were sick in body; others were sick in soul. But they all needed to know about the saving love of Jesus. God was not hindered by my weakened, sick body. All he wanted was my willingness, and his power did the rest! He brought great good out of my horrible illness.

Heavenly Father, thank you for using my sick body to portray your power and love in ways I would never be able to imagine! Thank you for transforming seemingly worthless situations into dynamic opportunities. Amen.

—*mm*

Will I Be Single Forever?

 "Fear not . . . for your Creator will be your husband. The Lord Almighty is his name! He is your Redeemer, the Holy One of Israel, the God of all the earth" (Isaiah 54:4-5, NLT).

The natural fear experienced by single people who live with debilitating fatigue is, *Will this condition prevent me from getting married?* We know how hard it is to do the normal things in life—caring for ourselves, getting out, fixing a meal—and we wonder if we could ever have the energy to have a meaningful relationship. As we see our friends getting married all around us, we cannot help but wonder whether anyone could ever love us enough to accept our disability and spend the rest of his or her life with us. We long for a husband or a wife with whom we can share ourselves and have an intimate relationship.

During the times when we feel the pain and loneliness of being single while dealing with our physical limitations, God wants us to look to him as our soul mate. By calling himself our "husband" in these verses from Isaiah 54, God shows us that he understands that aspect of our suffering. He knows the desires we have, and he wants to fill that void with his all-encompassing love.

Until God chooses to bless us with an earthly spouse, those of us who are single can spend time getting to know him as our husband. The Bible is the love letter he wrote to us, and by reading it, we can understand the heart of a compassionate, caring, personal God, who longs to know us in an intimate way. And we can respond to his written words by speaking to him openly through prayer and by writing back to him through journaling.

Being single is not necessarily easy, especially if we struggle with crippling fatigue. We long for someone to come into our lives, to love us even though we are not whole, and to be willing to grow old with us. But, until God sends that person to us, we can look to God our Creator to be our "Redeemer" from the loneliness of singlehood.

Dear Lover of my soul, please fill the void I feel in my heart. I long to be married, yet I feel as if this illness disqualifies me. Help me to long for you, to see you as my husband. Amen.

—cs

Rest for the Weary

 "Then Jesus said, 'Come to me, all of you who are weary and carry heavy burdens, and I will give you rest. Take my yoke upon you. Let me teach you, because I am humble and gentle, and you will find rest for your souls. For my yoke fits perfectly, and the burden I give you is light'" (Matthew 11:28-30, NLT).

As I read these verses, I identify with the one who is weary and burdened, but the last thing I want is more rest. I have to rest before an event. I have to rest after an event. Sometimes even that isn't enough, and I must miss the event altogether.

This ongoing fatigue controls my life. It doesn't seem to get better when I sleep or spend days in bed. It forces me to prioritize things, like whether to make dinner or wash my hair, when I used to do both without giving it another thought. Some days I struggle to think clearly and put my thoughts together. Some days it's just too much work even to talk to a friend. I feel very undependable. It frustrates me that I can never promise to take on a commitment without saying "unless I'm too tired."

These verses remind us that God's offer of rest is for our weary, burdened souls, our inner person. Through trials and struggles that come through his hand into our lives, he asks us to grow in our knowledge of him. He wants us to learn from him and learn about his yoke, which is handcarved to fit us perfectly.

The more we learn of Jesus' character and of his heart, the more we learn to trust him with our lives. The more we trust him, the more our souls will find the rest we seek. Maybe the circumstances won't change. Maybe we will still battle fatigue. But perhaps in the process, we will have tapped into the rest that Jesus promised for our souls.

Dear Yoke Maker, thank you that I may bring you my weariness and my burdens and in exchange accept the yoke you have asked me to wear. May I wear it with grace. Amen.

—*hg*

Finding Strength in Weakness

 "In the same way, the Spirit helps us in our weakness. We do not know what we ought to pray, but the Spirit himself intercedes for us with groans that words cannot express. And he who searches our hearts knows the mind of the Spirit, because the Spirit intercedes for the saints in accordance with God's will" (Romans 8:26-27, NIV).

I am not where I chose to be. I chose career, yet have been disabled over twelve years. I chose family, but I now have no husband or children. I chose athletic recreation, yet I must force myself to walk or exercise daily for symptom management. I did not choose chronic pain, yet the pain screams moment by moment, hour by hour, day by day. I demand to know why. Surely God could find a better use for me as an energetic career woman than as a chronic pain patient whose days are exhausted with doctors' appointments.

My strength fails me, and I am discouraged. Pain alienates and isolates me. Sleep does not refresh. My concentration is impaired. My ability to predict my pain level or control the pain is unpredictable.

But what is predictable is that God has sent his Spirit to help me in the midst of my weakness. God's Holy Spirit prays for me when I can find no words. And, these verses tell us, the Holy Spirit knows God's will and prays for us in harmony with that will.

What is humanly impossible is divinely accomplished. I pray that God will remove my pain, but even more important, I pray that I will follow his will for me. While a lifetime of pain is a fearful prospect, I am content and trust God to use my pain as an instrument of his healing love in another person's life. Whether God uses me to support, guide, or teach another, my strength comes clearly, unquestionably, and totally from him—in spite of, or because of, the pain.

Dear heavenly Father, thank you for coming to me in the midst of my weakness and giving me strength through the presence of your Holy Spirit. Thank you that the Spirit prays on my behalf and will ensure that I am in harmony with your will. Amen.

—ns

Why Won't I Rest?

 "The Lord is my shepherd, I shall not be in want.
He makes me lie down in green pastures,
he leads me beside quiet waters" (Psalm 23:1-3, NIV).

These comforting verses of the Twenty-third Psalm were the first Scripture verses I memorized when I was a small child. Through many dark hours these verses have provided me with comfort. Recently, however, I realized that they also reveal something very fundamental about God.

Before I was struck by a disabling illness, my life had been an exciting, nonstop whirlwind of fulfilling activity. Then suddenly I was confined to the couch, a reluctant patient who longed for activity and interaction. "Think of it as a forced sabbatical," a caring friend told me after hearing my diagnosis. It was good advice, but for an energetic extrovert, it was not easy advice to follow. The last thing I wanted was a sabbatical.

Despite weakness and pain, I fought being bedridden. On days when I could get up, I used all my energy, despite the fact that people repeatedly told me to pace myself and to schedule periods of rest before

I felt totally exhausted. In spite of these warnings, I found that I simply could not give myself permission to rest or relax without feeling a sense of guilt or shame. I had spent so many years being active and productive that I honestly didn't know how to rest.

It is in these familiar verses from Psalm 23 that we can find some refreshing insight: *The Lord is my shepherd.* Think about what it means to be watched over and cared for by a shepherd who was willing to lay down his life for us. *He makes me lie down in green pastures, he leads me beside quiet waters.* God not only gives us permission to rest, but knowing our deeper needs and having our best interests in mind, he *commands* us to rest!

Misplaced guilt can lead us in the opposite direction, away from the lush green pastures and the soul-restoring waters that God provides for each of us according to our need. God does not seek endless productivity but seeks our willingness to trust and follow him wherever he leads us.

Lord Jesus, gentle Shepherd, thank you for loving me and knowing my needs. Thank you for making me rest and for leading me to where you can restore me in body and soul. Amen.
—*lvv*

Content with Weakness?

 "Therefore I am well content with weaknesses, with insults, with distresses, with persecutions, with difficulties, for Christ's sake; for when I am weak, then am I strong" (2 Corinthians 12:10, NASB).

In the apostle Paul's early years, he lived an easy life. A Pharisee from the tribe of Benjamin, he was a respected teacher and scholar. He was well known because of the number of Christians he persecuted.

But then Paul met God, and his life changed drastically. He began preaching about Christ to the very people who had paid him to murder Christians. As a result he was constantly imprisoned, stoned, and beaten. He suffered slander, sleeplessness, hunger, and poverty on a regular basis. In addition to all this, Paul struggled with a physical disability that God chose not to heal even though Paul prayed desperately for its removal. Despite these overwhelming circumstances Paul could say that he was content with weakness (2 Cor. 12:10).

The secret of Paul's contentment was in his purpose for living. In several of his letters he articulates that purpose: "For to me, to live is

Christ" (Phil. 1:21, NIV); "I want to know Christ" (Phil. 3:10, NIV); "I consider everything a loss compared to the surpassing greatness of knowing Christ Jesus my Lord" (Phil. 3:8, NIV).

Paul's goal in life was *knowing* Christ—not preaching Christ or performing miracles for Christ or even making disciples for Christ. Paul's pursuit of this goal was never swayed by changing circumstances. Paul was content in prison or at a prayer meeting, famished or full, penniless or prosperous.

If we lose our job or our spouse, if we're confined to a wheelchair or a bed, we can find the sweet peace of contentment as long as our purpose for living is knowing Christ. Paul urged us to follow his example of single-mindedness. Only then can the glow of the world fade away and the pain of circumstances soften. Only then can we agree that when we are weak, then we are strong.

Lord, help me to find contentment in knowing you, even if that means I will stay physically weak with illness. Help me to know you deeply. Help me to know not just your power but also your suffering. Amen.

—*rr*

Don't Despise Those Who Are Weak

"Let me teach you, because I am humble and gentle" (Matthew 11:29, NLT).

In a culture that glorifies strength and vitality, it is easy to despise weakness. We are surrounded by visions of youth and beauty. Athletes become cultural gods, and fitness is practically a religion. In such a culture, it is easy for those of us who are physically weak to feel a sense of shame and failure because we are not able to do the things physically strong people can do.

God, however, shows us repeatedly in his Word that strength and might do not always win the day. We see it vividly in 1 Samuel in the account of David and Goliath. A young shepherd overcomes a giant Philistine warrior. Similarly, Gideon, who was the least in his family and whose clan was the weakest in Manasseh, defeated the mighty Midian army with only three hundred men (Judg. 6:15).

God does not despise weakness. He is a God who prefers lambs to wolves, who values gentleness over aggression, who calls the meek and lowly blessed, and who shows us that brokenness is a place of spiritual potency. The Source of all strength does not hold our weakness in contempt. Why, then, should we?

In spite of what we are led to believe by advertisers and the media, we do not have to have perfect bodies and perfect health to be perfectly happy and fulfilled. Rather we need to keep our focus on God, our source of strength. Through physical suffering and weakness we are given the opportunity to learn to trust God, to accept his grace, and to rely on his limitless strength rather than our own unreliable resources. As David and Gideon discovered, when we embrace our vulnerability, we discover God's strength. Only then can God be our refuge and our might, our ever-present help in trouble.

Loving Father, you are the all-powerful king of the universe and yet you are gentle and humble. Help me, Lord, to keep my mind focused on your definition of strength rather than what our culture would have me believe. Amen.

—*lvv*

Jesus Understands

"Therefore, it was necessary for Jesus to be in every respect like us, his brothers and sisters, so that he could be our merciful and faithful High Priest before God. He then could offer a sacrifice that would take away the sins of the people. Since he himself has gone through suffering and temptation, he is able to help us when we are being tempted" (Hebrews 2:17-18, NLT).

I am a teenager, and I have struggled with pain and fatigue for several years. Many times I feel that no one understands what it's like to have life destroyed by chronic illness. My teachers and friends at school don't understand why I can't be there every day. They don't understand why I have to say no to so many things. They will never be able to understand the pain I have battled over the years.

I remember lying in the hospital with severe migraines and seizures. I needed some relief, but the neurologist who was treating me told my mom to take me home because he claimed I was faking being sick. Talk about being misunderstood! I felt alone and betrayed.

Someone sent me a comforting card with the words from Hebrews 2:17-18. Those verses remind me that Jesus understands our human limitations. He suffered, too. He knows what it is like to feel alone and betrayed. That makes me feel close to him.

Jesus has also struggled with weakness. In Hebrews 5:2 it says that "he is able to deal gently with the people, though they are ignorant and wayward. For he is subject to the same weaknesses they have" (NLT). Even Jesus felt that no one understood his experience. Jesus did what we need to do: He turned to his Father in heaven. The next time you feel that no one understands what you are going through, look to heaven. Jesus understands.

Lord Jesus, thank you for suffering the way you did when you lived on earth. Thank you that you felt so many of the same things we feel as humans. When I feel alone and betrayed, I take comfort in knowing that you understand me and that you will help me. Amen.

—av

The Fellowship of Suffering

 "I want to know Christ and the power of his resurrection and the fellowship of sharing in his sufferings, becoming like him in his death" (Philippians 3:10, NIV).

Throughout my life, this verse from Philippians 3 has taken on increasingly deeper significance. When I was a young girl, I was stirred deeply by the realization we can know Christ better and live our lives in the power of his resurrection. Yet, as only an adolescent can, I quickly quoted past the "sharing in the sufferings, becoming like him in his death" phrases, somehow confident that I could enjoy the power without having to endure the suffering.

Now, many years later, the significance of having chosen this Scripture passage as my life verse has not eluded me. The Lord has asked me to make this verse truly mine, quoting it again, slowly, through the next phrase: "and the fellowship of sharing in his sufferings."

Fellowship forged through shared suffering creates a unique relationship. A strong, personal, and comforting bond develops. That bond is cast and molded through the heat of pain.

We who suffer from debilitating fatigue and illness have the opportunity to experience that bond with Jesus by reaching out, taking his hand, and walking through this thing together. We can take comfort in his presence, knowing that he has walked this way before us.

In a very real sense you and I also walk this path together—a community of fellow sufferers, sharing in his sufferings. We unwaveringly hold each other in our hearts, reaching out in love whenever God gives strength and opportunity. Suffering with Jesus leads directly to community—a community that has been given a special ability to care deeply for each other. Has God put someone who is suffering in your path? Don't miss the shared joy of fellowship in suffering. Laugh and pray and cry together. "Then," as Thomas Kelley says, "strength, given to them by God, becomes our strength, and our joy, given to us by God, becomes their joy."

Suffering Savior, my heart is comforted in the midst of this suffering because through it I have come to fellowship with you as my friend. Amen.
—ph

Too Tired to Do the Job

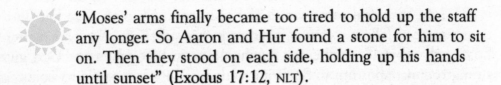

"Moses' arms finally became too tired to hold up the staff any longer. So Aaron and Hur found a stone for him to sit on. Then they stood on each side, holding up his hands until sunset" (Exodus 17:12, NLT).

My years of battling with fatigue have been complicated by the reality that our daughter was also severely debilitated by the same fatiguing illness. I have often said that I don't know what is harder: to be the sick person or to be the mother of a sick person. Obviously, I can't separate the two, but I think that it is much harder to be the mother of a debilitated child.

Many days I could hardly handle the basics of my own life, let alone the needs our daughter had for physical help or comfort or companionship. Like Moses, I finally became too tired to do the job any longer.

And just as God faithfully nudged Aaron and Hur to help Moses, he also sent me helpers to hold up my arms in the battle. Friends drove our daughter to school if she felt well enough to attend for a few hours.

Some brought her books from their children's libraries. Others video-taped children's classics for her to watch when she was too sick to read. Still others came to lie on the floor with her and play a board game or read a book to her.

When we feel that we are too tired to do the job, God can provide help to us in the form of neighbors who loan us a book or church friends who bring in a meal or family members who come in to vacuum a floor for us. Who are the Aarons and the Hurs whom God has sent to you over the years? How have they supported you in the battle? How can you thank them for their part in helping you in your struggle?

Lord, thank you that when you called me to a battle, you also sent people to support me in the process. Thank you for the people whom you have nudged to hold up my arms for me when I have been too tired to do the job. Amen.
    —lv

Made More Sensitive

 "He was despised and rejected—a man of sorrows, acquainted with bitterest grief. We turned our backs on him and looked the other way when he went by. He was despised, and we did not care. Yet it was our weaknesses he carried; it was our sorrows that weighed him down. And we thought his troubles were a punishment from God for his own sins! But he was wounded and crushed for our sins. He was beaten that we might have peace. He was whipped, and we were healed!" (Isaiah 53:3-5, NLT).

God can offer us comfort when we suffer not just because he loves us but because he knows firsthand what it feels like to be a human and to suffer physical pain. Through the mystery of the Incarnation, God became a man, vulnerable to bumps, bruises, headaches, fatigue, just like you and me. He knows the agony of protracted torture and the emotional pain of being rejected, despised, and misunderstood.

Jesus showed us that suffering does not need to make us into bitter victims of circumstance. Rather we can allow our experience to make us more compassionate and skillful in comforting others in their distress. In his book *Unto the Hills*, Billy Graham says, "To have suffered much is like knowing many languages. It gives the sufferer access to many more people." Our capacity to comfort and to encourage increases the more we suffer.

The many symptoms that accompany our fatiguing illness give us access not only to fellow sufferers with the same mystifying symptoms but also to anyone who is physically weak or in pain: the elderly, the dying, even a friend with a twenty-four-hour virus. If we allow ourselves to become ministers instead of moaners, God can use our illness to make us powerful intercessors and sensitive comforters.

Lord Jesus, you loved us so much that you came down from heaven and took on a human body to take away our sins and draw us closer to you. Use my illness to make me a more effective witness of your love and grace, and use me to help encourage and comfort those who are struggling. Amen.
    —*lvv*

Strength for the Long Haul

 "We also pray that you will be strengthened with his glorious power so that you will have all the patience and endurance you need" (Colossians 1:11, NLT).

One of the hardest things I faced in dealing with fatigue is that it was chronic; it didn't go away. Every day I had to muster the emotional and spiritual energy to cope with a body drained of physical strength. I found that the coping skills I had developed over the years for dealing with short crises were not sufficient for dealing with this long-term situation.

Even though I never doubted that God was with me, I often struggled to remain hopeful. My confidence in his presence would be strong for a while, but then it would fade, leaving me increasingly insecure and fearful. I needed strength for the long haul.

Maybe you have had the same experience. At times you feel confident that you will make it through the long months and years, but then something happens and you lose hope.

We can find comfort and perspective in remembering that people whom we consider to be heroes of the faith also needed strength for the long haul. It has always struck me that after God told Abraham that he would be the father of many nations, it was twenty-five years before that promise began to be fulfilled. In that twenty-five-year period, God did not visit Abraham every other month to assure him that he remembered who he was and that he would fulfill the promise. In that long stretch of time, God spoke to Abraham about the promise only five times. The rest of the time Abraham had to be confident in God's word.

Noah had a similar experience. After God told Noah to build the ark, Noah began the work. But it was a hundred twenty years later that God finally sent Noah and his family into the ark. Noah's faith needed patience and endurance to last for the long haul.

God is not asking us to hang on for a hundred twenty years or even for twenty-five years. But if he did, he would give us the same endurance that he gave to Abraham and to Noah.

Lord, help me to stay confident in you for the long haul. Thank you that you give me patience and endurance to wait through the long months and years. You are faithful. Amen.
    —lv

Power to the Weary

"He gives power to those who are tired and worn out; he offers strength to the weak" (Isaiah 40:29, NLT).

Tired. Worn out. Those are just two terms that describe what I experienced when I first became ill with CFIDS. In fact, adequately descriptive words were hard to find. *Exhausted. Depleted. Sapped.* These didn't seem to get even close to capturing the significant drain I felt in those early years.

I had never had a chronic illness before, and I was not prepared for the way this one sapped me emotionally and spiritually as well as physically. I felt so empty, and I didn't know how I would ever fill my reserves again to face another day.

Have you felt drained like that too? Have you wondered if you would be able to go on? The words from Isaiah 40 comfort us. They tell us that the Lord promises to give power to those who are tired and worn out, to those who can't go on.

As I look back on the last ten years, I can see that God has given me strength and power. I didn't see it as power at the time, but I did have the strength to be a faithful spouse. I had the strength to be an effective parent. I had the strength to rest. I had the strength to develop a growing faith in God. I had the strength to be a listening friend. When I think about it, that's pretty powerful.

How does God give power to you when you are tired and worn out? How has he offered you strength? In the coming days look for ways that he gives you power and strength when you are too exhausted to go on.

Powerful Lord, you look at my tired and worn body and soul, and you touch me with your strength. Thank you for sustaining me. Help me to see your power at work within me, even in the midst of debilitation. Amen.
—*lv*

Too Tired to Read the Bible

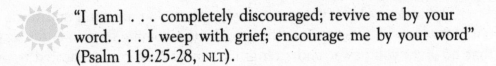 "I [am] . . . completely discouraged; revive me by your word. . . . I weep with grief; encourage me by your word" (Psalm 119:25-28, NLT).

In the years of dealing with a disabling illness, I have had many questions and many decisions to make. Some days I am so deeply discouraged that I feel as if I am walking around in darkness. If ever I needed the light of God's Word to direct me, it is now.

God promised that he will direct our tired steps down the right path through his Word, but how can God's Word guide me when I'm too tired some days to read it? The illness with which I struggle causes such brain fog that some days I can barely assimilate the words in the Bible, let alone have a sustained time of meditation. Other days even if I read it, my mind can't think clearly. Verses I memorized years ago can't be recalled. How can I find new ways to allow God's Word to revive and encourage me?

Some days listening to a song or reading a hymn from a hymnbook can remind me of his love and care. Other days, when my mind is not focusing well, a children's Bible version of the Bible that is easier to read and understand may help. Reading God's Word in a devotional book like this one can help my mind focus on him as I share emotions and struggles with others who have walked through times of fatigue and trials. That helps me feel that I am not alone. It also keeps me from self-pity as I see the specific circumstances other people face as they walk on their part of the path.

Other times God's Word revives me as I hear a teaching tape or a Christian radio broadcast. When my mind and emotions are weak, these activities strengthen and refresh me.

In various ways God's Word can penetrate the brain fog and touch our hearts with hope and comfort and direction. Let's continue to explore ways to let God's Word touch our lives.

Creator God, help me to hear your voice when fatigue seems to overwhelm me. Thank you that your Holy Spirit can teach me through a variety of means. Thank you for offering me light on my journey, strength in my weakness. Amen.

   —hg

Hope in God

 "Why am I discouraged? Why so sad? I will put my hope in God! I will praise him again—my Savior and my God" (Psalm 43:5, NLT).

When the psalmist David was in despair, he put his hope in God. He spoke confidently of God as his Savior. When trials stretch us, in whom or in what do we hope?

My hope was challenged when I suffered symptoms that no one could understand. Each time I had tests done and the doctors said, "We don't know what is causing your symptoms," I would collapse in sobs. The doctors knew I was horribly sick. I could hardly function. Yet they could find no source for the symptoms. In the midst of this confusion, I lost hope very quickly.

Some of you may be facing that same situation. If you do not have a diagnosis for what is causing your pain and debilitation, then there is no prognosis, no specific treatment, no support group, and—worst of all—no hope for a cure. What are you to do? How do you cope? The words of the psalmist echo your questions and the response of faith: "And so, Lord, where do I put my hope? My only hope is in you" (Psalm 39:7, NLT).

It is natural to hope in the visible things: medication, surgery, treatment, or a physician. But when we can no longer hope in these, we can find comfort in God. The psalmist reminds us, "Find rest, O my soul, in God alone; my hope comes from him. He alone is my rock and salvation; he is my fortress, I will not be shaken" (Psalm 62:5-6, NIV). When things fail, we are shaken! But God will not fail us. We can place our unreserved hope in him.

In the midst of our discouragement, confusion, and sadness, we can trust God's grace to sustain us, his love to comfort us, and his peace to stabilize us. He is worthy of our hope.

Father, you are my only hope. You are all I have and all that I need. Thank you for reminding me of this precious truth day by day. Amen.
 —mm

Choose to Live

"For to me, living is for Christ, and dying is even better. Yet if I live, that means fruitful service for Christ. I really don't know which is better. I'm torn between two desires: Sometimes I want to live, and sometimes I long to go and be with Christ. That would be far better for me, but it is better for you that I live. I am convinced of this, so I will continue with you so that you will grow and experience the joy of your faith" (Philippians 1:21-25, NLT).

Sometimes I am so sick and so full of pain that I wish I could die. Nothing seems to help. Life just doesn't seem worth living. Maybe you have never come to this point in your battle, but I know of many people who share my struggle. I know in my head that taking my own life is wrong, but my desire to be beyond the pain and suffering is so great that I just wish I could begin my life in heaven.

When I have those feelings, I need people to remind me that life is worth living. Because the apostle Paul had similar thoughts, his words have helped me keep perspective. While he was in the Philippian jail, he thought about the advantages of life and death. If he were to die, he would be with Christ and his suffering would end. That had its advantages to him. But if he were to live, he could continue to proclaim the good news of Jesus' resurrection from the dead to those who had not yet heard of it and he could bring joy to the lives of his fellow believers. That was even better.

Each day, as we face thoughts of life and death, let's choose to live, trusting that God will use us—and our willingness to surrender our sick bodies to his purposes—to touch the lives of other people.

Dear Lord, when I am so full of pain that I want to die, help me to choose to live. Use my choice to live to benefit other suffering people. Thank you that you take the difficult experiences in my life and turn them into good. Amen.
    —cs

He Promises Peace

 "The Lord, your Redeemer, the Holy One of Israel, says: I am the Lord your God, who teaches you what is good and leads you along the paths you should follow. Oh, that you had listened to my commands! Then you would have had peace flowing like a gentle river and righteousness rolling like waves" (Isaiah 48:17-18, NLT).

In the midst of the chaos of a life turned upside down by a debilitating chronic illness, I have come to sense a greater need for God's peace. I long for the kind of peace—well-being (*shalom* in Hebrew) and harmony (*irene* in Greek)—that this passage from Isaiah describes.

It is important to remember that peace is not the absence of conflict—whose life on earth will ever be free of conflict?—but the steady inner assurance that God is at the center of our lives. He is the gentle river that will carry us.

I have an uneasy feeling that many of us feel that following God's commands means that we must accomplish certain things. Those of us who highly value planning and action sometimes find ourselves on the river of God's will rowing vigorously upstream. We focus our energy on doing all sorts of good things. As Sybil Stanton explains in *The 25-Hour Woman:* "I have a strong hunch that when we meet our Maker, we will breathlessly parade our noble activities, and he might well burst our busy bubble with a simple comment: 'I never expected you to do all that.'"

Are we willing to lay down the oars and rest, allowing the gentle current of the Spirit to take us where God wants us to go? By aligning our will with his, we can forge a partnership that opens the floodgates of peace. In sickness our life can reflect the harmony he longs to bring—as deep and as wide as a river.

Dear Lord, how I long for your peace. I know that apart from you, inner peace is as illusive as physical health. I desire to listen and follow your commands. I trust you for the courage to lay down the oars and cooperate in the working out of your good purposes in my life. Amen.
   —*ph*

That Saved a Wretch like Me

"For it is by grace you have been saved" (Ephesians 2:8, NIV).

Many of you may recognize the title of this meditation as a line from the hymn "Amazing Grace," one of the most beloved Christian songs ever written. These few words, so simple yet so powerful, capture the essence of our faith by relaying the concept that we cannot experience the grace, or unmerited favor, of God unless we are aware of our own sin.

Unfortunately, in our culture, which worships self-actualization, self-empowerment, and self-help, the concept that we are totally and completely wretched is dismissed as destructive and uncaring. We who are chronically ill, however, know better. There is nothing that strips away the veneer of self-righteousness quicker than long-term illness. Through our illnesses, we are forced to confront our baser emotions such as bitterness, envy, despair. I am often too sick to be civil, or even polite, let alone pretend that I am some wonderful person.

From the moment we think ourselves deserving or worthy of

God's grace and favor, we lose the ability to receive it. This illness has taught me that without God, I am totally and completely helpless, incapable of being the kind of person I want to be. But because of this illness, I can understand and cherish God's grace in ways that most healthy people will never be able to.

In the apostle Paul's letter to the church at Rome, he tells us that where sin increases, grace increases all the more (Rom 5:20). That is because only through our increased awareness of our own sinful natures are we able to receive all the blessings that our gracious God has for us. And no one knew that better than the author of "Amazing Grace." May we, like him, learn to say, "I once was lost but now am found, was blind but now I see."

Lord, you are gracious and compassionate, slow to anger and abounding in love! Thank you that you do not treat me as my sin deserves. Help me to open my hands to receive your grace, which strengthens me. Amen.

—*gf*

Is There Someone Special for Me?

 "Trust in the Lord with all your heart; do not depend on your own understanding. Seek his will in all you do, and he will direct your paths" (Proverbs 3:5-6, NLT).

I have been sick and debilitated for most of my life. In my teen years and my early twenties, I often asked God, "Will you ever send me a husband, someone who can cope with my limitations?" God's answer to me was this passage from Proverbs 3: *Trust me.*

God tells us to trust him with all our hearts. It is very difficult to trust him when we are ill and alone and see no evidence of his working on our behalf. I prayed for years for a husband but remained single. I know what it is like to suffer *alone*, to go to the doctor's office *alone*, and to lie in a hospital bed *alone*, and to be in pain *alone*. I know how it feels to be without the comfort of a spouse, longing to be held. I know how it feels to face the hard medical decisions *alone* and to face the staggering medical bills *alone*.

God also tells us not to trust our own understanding of the situation. When I looked at my life logically, I concluded that I would *never* be married. I knew marriage takes a lot of work, and I had seen healthy couples who could not make it work. Who was I to think that I could sustain a marriage while I was ill? But ill health does not frustrate God's will for our lives.

God works differently in each one of our lives. For my dear friend who lives with daily pain and fatigue, God gave the abiding power of his presence. She testifies to having peace and genuine joy. But God's will for me was different. Twenty years after college, God brought into my life a husband whom he had prepared for the care I would require. The twenty years of waiting gave me the opportunity to experience the reality of God's faithfulness to all those who seek his will in all they do.

I share my story to encourage you that in whatever circumstances you find yourself, you can trust God's good purposes for you. Give him your whole heart. Seek him in everything you do. He will do the rest.

Dear Lord, thank you that I can trust you with all of my heart. Thanks that your purposes for me are beyond my understanding. Give me peace as I face the future. Amen.

 —*mm*

Laughter, the Natural Healer

 "A cheerful heart is good medicine, but a broken spirit saps a person's strength" (Proverbs 17:22, NLT).

We who are chronically ill and fatigued often have a difficult time seeing anything humorous about our lives. Too quickly we begin to focus on our problems, and everything becomes serious.

I am blessed with three people who have kept me laughing during the years of my illness. My youngest daughter, who was born with a smile on her face, has the gift of making lemonade out of lemons; she has often taught me how to make a refreshing drink out of my sour situation. My mother has shared with me not only her unflagging sense of humor but also her unstoppable spirit in the face of her own trials with diabetes, three heart attacks, and triple bypass surgery. I can also always count on my neighbor to make me laugh when we talk on the phone.

These three people are an effective prescription for me. They cheer my heart and help me keep perspective. God wants us to have a merry heart and to laugh. Recent studies have shown that laughter actually facilitates the healing process in our immune systems. Biological processes are activated when we laugh heartily. Laughter reduces stress and releases endorphins, which give us a feeling of well-being.

Who are the people who can give you the medicine of laughter? Spend time with them. Talk with them on the phone. Don't take your situation so seriously that you don't take time to laugh. Or maybe we should say, take your situation seriously enough to find time to laugh.

If funny friends are not available, rent them—at least rent a funny movie. Tape humorous television programs, and then let yourself laugh. It is good medicine.

Dear God, help me to find the humor in my life. Bring into my life people and situations that will cause me to laugh and feel cheerful, even when I may not feel like laughing. Then help me to spread laughter and bring cheer into someone else's life. Amen.

—cf

Waiting on Him—Alone

 "I wait for the Lord, my soul waits, and in his word I put my hope" (Psalm 130:5, NIV).

There is a certain amount of aloneness that accompanies any illness. Suddenly life as we knew it comes to a screeching halt, while those around us continue to sprint, cheered along by a society that values a fast pace. Sometimes we search for a new community that will help alleviate the loneliness. But people seldom slow down. The new community does not fill the vacuum, and we are still alone, waiting.

At first we are afraid of that waiting, of that aloneness. It threatens us. Our natural tendency is to search for ways to "catch up" with those on ahead, hoping someone will slow down enough to walk with us at our pace. But that does not often happen, and we are left waiting.

Maybe the waiting and the aloneness are part of God's plan. In the same way that the doctor may prescribe "aggressive rest therapy" for our bodies, God may be prescribing "aggressive alone therapy" for our souls. In our times of aloneness and waiting, we may discover, as David Seamands did, that "God wants to teach us full dependence on himself through the discipline of detachment from others."

As gifts from God sent to nourish and strengthen our souls, solitude and silence begin the waiting process. Silence becomes a creative space in which we regain perspective on the whole. We begin to realize that this illness has a deeper meaning: this secluded, quiet, lonely place is our desert. In *A Center of Quiet*, David Runcorn reflects with us: "It is hard to believe that this silent, shadowy wasteland could be the home of the Spirit, concealing the deepest springs of God's life and our security. Surely this is a place to avoid, rather than to journey further into."

The waiting—for God to reveal himself to us, for our souls to find their home—is worth the loneliness. The prophet Isaiah reminds us, "In quietness and trust is your strength. . . . Blessed are all who wait for him" (Isa. 30:15, 18, NIV).

Lord of the silence, give me the courage to embrace the solitude and the aloneness. Teach me to hope in your Word as I wait for you—alone. Amen.
　　—*ph*

Don't Give Up

 "'For I know the plans I have for you,' says the Lord. 'They are plans for good and not for disaster, to give you a future and a hope'" (Jeremiah 29:11, NLT).

When I first fell ill, I was convinced I would bounce back quickly. After all, God had opened so many doors for me. He had brought me all the way to Africa to work with the rural poor. He had even provided a Sunday school class of eager teenagers at the multinational church where my husband and I worshiped. I felt needed, appreciated, and fulfilled. I felt that I was finally doing what God had created me to do. Surely, I reasoned, God wouldn't let this illness continue.

When I did not recover, I was consumed with frustration. Plans and programs were put on the shelf. Ministry opportunities went unrealized. "Lord," I cried, "what is happening? Wasn't this life of ministry your will for me? There is so much left to do! Please heal me so that I can get back to your plan for my life!"

In the book of Jeremiah, we find the people of Judah in a similar situation. Held captive in Babylon, they are eager to return to Jerusalem and ready to believe the false prophets who promised quick fixes to their problems. God spoke to them through his prophet Jeremiah, telling them to be patient and promising to bring them back to Jerusalem in seventy years. God said to the people of Judah, "Don't give up. I have good plans for you. I don't intend to bring you disaster. I have planned for you a hopeful future. Just trust me."

Like the people of Judah, our vision can sometimes be limited. Rather than trusting God, who sees the big picture, we become impatient and are tempted to believe that he has abandoned us. Sometimes in our desire to serve God, we focus on what we want to do for him. Our response should be to believe his promises and trust him in spite of changing circumstances.

Dear Lord, forgive me for thinking you have given up on me. When things suddenly change course and the future looks unclear, help me to trust in you and to be assured that your plan for my life is good and full of hope. Amen.
    —lvv

Why the Little We Can Do Is Enough

 "For the Lord will go ahead of you, and the God of Israel will protect you from behind" (Isaiah 52:12, NLT).

As the children of Israel tramped through the wilderness, they depended on a pillar of cloud that went in front of them and the angel of God who stood behind them. On that long, dusty trip through what appeared to be a God-forsaken desert, God's people were literally in the center of his will. God was the vanguard and the rear guard of this difficult trek.

We, too, are passing through a desert, where sometimes just putting one foot in front of the other seems impossible. Author Amy Carmichael, a missionary to India, understood what that felt like. A fall in the dark, a sprain of an ankle, and—after years of caring for and serving others—she suddenly found herself confined to her bed with crippling symptoms. Unable to perform the many tasks that she had done before the accident, she did not give up. She knew that when the Lord gives us something to do, he promises to go before us and come along behind us, preparing the way ahead and tying up the loose ends from behind. In her devotional *The Edges of His Ways*, she says: "If he gathers us up, he gathers up also the things we have dropped, our poor fallen resolutions, mistakes, everything, and deals with them himself."

While in the past we may have been able to take on and complete a large, detailed project, now we may have barely enough stamina to start, much less finish, a small task. Suddenly we find we are paralyzed. Believing that it is irresponsible to start something we cannot finish, we hesitate to get involved in anything until we are confident we are up to completing the task.

But God reminds us that he goes ahead of us and behind us, gathering up the things we have dropped, as Amy Carmichael puts it. That promise can give us courage to step out in faith and do what God asks us to do, even though we do not know how we will complete the task. Surrounded by his loving support, we can take that first step. He will take care of the rest.

Dear Lord, I take this next step in faith, realizing I do not have the strength to continue this journey alone. I am trusting totally in you and the promise of your all-encompassing presence, encouragement, and support. Amen.

—*ph*

Wrapped in God's Comfort

 "Praise be to the God and Father of our Lord Jesus Christ, the Father of compassion and the God of all comfort, who comforts us in all our troubles, so that we can comfort those in any trouble with the comfort we ourselves have received from God" (2 Corinthians 1:3-4, NIV).

I live in the Washington, D.C., area, where people's value is often judged by what they do. When people meet for the first time, they ask "Where do you work?" or "What do you do?" Those routine questions became embarrassing for me when I looked healthy but was unable to work. Not to hold a salaried position and earn a regular paycheck were devastating losses. Much later, to my surprise and shame, I realized that I had secretly "bought into" the cultural bias. My own sense of worth had become rooted in what I did: my profession.

When I became disabled, I isolated myself from my peers and neighbors. Averse even to being seen by colleagues, I would not walk outside during commuting hours. Until I could resume my career, I felt like dead weight.

After I suffered years of alienation, God in his mercy drew me into the fellowship of a loving church where Christians accepted my deficits and unique strengths. They supported and encouraged me as a member of the body of Christ. By including me, making room for my participation, facilitating my attendance, and especially undergirding me with their prayer support, they were vehicles of God's comfort and demonstrations of Christ's love in action.

God's comfort and love for us do not depend on our professional status. He loves us because of who he is: the God of all comfort. Our worth and comfort are found only in him.

Beyond that he allows us to be his hands and voice of comfort in the lives of others. The comfort that God has shown me through his people is the comfort I can share with others in their isolation, discouragement, and suffering.

God of all comfort, thank you that your comfort reaches me in all my troubles, whether I am in a prominent position or bedridden. Help me to comfort others with the comfort you have shown to me. Amen.

—ns

Follow the Son

"Your word is a lamp for my feet
   and a light for my path.
I've promised it once, and I'll promise again:
   I will obey your wonderful laws.
I have suffered much, O Lord;
   restore my life again, just as you promised.
Lord, accept my grateful thanks
   and teach me your laws" (Psalm 119:105-8, NLT).

Recently I read that the face of a sunflower constantly follows the sun. In my mind's eye, I could see a vivid yellow sunflower with its brown center very slowly shifting its face to follow the light of the sun as it made its path across the sky.

There is a lesson in the flower's action. During this time of fatigue in our lives, we can turn our faces upward and *follow the Son*—the Son of God. We can focus on the light of God's Word and follow it. Every day we can intentionally spend time reading his Word, even if we can concentrate only on one verse. That one verse may be exactly what we need to give us the strength to make it through the challenges of that particular day.

During the first year of my battle with CFIDS, I felt as if God's door was shut and he was nowhere to be found. I felt abandoned and alone. Because of my faith in God, I knew that even though I could not feel his presence, he had promised to be with me. To encourage myself, I wrote Romans 4:20-21 on a note card and taped it where I could see it on the headboard of my bed: "Abraham never wavered in believing God's promise. In fact, his faith grew stronger, and in this he brought glory to God. He was absolutely convinced that God was able to do anything he promised" (NLT). These verses became my mainstay in a time of deep despair and depression as I grieved the loss of my health. As I allowed the light of those words to shine on me and as I followed that light, I grew in my confidence that God is able to do anything he promises.

Dear God, help me to be like the sunflower. Help me to focus my life on the light that you have given me in your Word. Help me to very confidently *follow the Son*. Amen.

    —*cf*

Meet the Writers

When the publishers asked me to write this book, I recognized that I did not have the energy to do it alone. But I knew people who could join me in sharing insights God has given in times of deep fatigue. The writers who have contributed to this book are people I met through writing my first book, *Finding Strength in Weakness: Hope and Help for Families Battling Chronic Fatigue Syndrome*. I chose these people because I knew they would not have glib responses to their situations, but I also knew that in the midst of their struggles; they had forged a faith that is vibrant, steady, and very real.

Candy Feathers (cf) has lived with chronic fatigue and immune dysfunction syndrome for nearly eight years and has found that humor does more to lift her spirits than anything else. Now that her four daughters are young adults, she has retired from her role as homeschool teacher.

Gregg Charles Fisher (gf), author of *Chronic Fatigue Syndrome: A Comprehensive Guide to Symptoms, Treatments, and Solving the Practical Problems of CFS*, has suffered for the past sixteen years. During those years he also cared for his wife, Shawn Fisher, who was seriously debilitated with the same illness for fifteen years. Gregg is now involved with the youth group ministry at their church.

Shawn Susan Fisher (sf) not only was disabled by chronic fatigue and immune dysfunction syndrome for fifteen years, but her husband, Gregg Fisher, battled the same illness during that time. Recently Shawn was miraculously healed by God, and she is now expecting their first child.

Helen Gruelle (hg), who has had CFIDS for more than ten years, has written about her experience with her illness in *Horizontal in a Vertical World*. When her energy permits, Helen—a wife, mother of four, and grandmother of three—paints in both watercolor and oil and teaches Bible studies.

Priscilla Hirst (ph) contracted chronic fatigue and immune dysfunction syndrome after a bout with typhoid in 1981. She and her family served as missionaries to Latin America from 1976 to 1993. On good days, Priscilla and her husband search used bookstores and libraries for spiritual-development books, which they use in their ministry of spiritual direction.

Jane Ellen Hodges (jeh) has lived for nearly five years with fatigue due to thyroid imbalances, CFIDS, and fibromyalgia. She is single and works part-time as a school nurse and part-time as a hospital nurse. She spent a year on the mission field.

Deborah McAdoo (dm) has lived with CFIDS for fifteen years. She is a wife, friend, counselor, worker, legal advocate, and prayer warrior.

Marilyn Marshall (mm) has lived the greater part of her life with debilitating pain and fatigue caused by an autoimmune intestinal disease. With sheer "guts" and determination, she practiced medical social work until her strength gave out. Now at home, she continues to minister to fellow sufferers in person, by phone, and through correspondence.

Barbara Masoner (bsm), a portrait artist, became ill in 1988 with what was later diagnosed as CFIDS. Barbara is involved with women's ministry at her church but is not able to paint, draw, read, or in any way be as active as she had always been. She finds maintaining relationships hard. Barbara shares her insights about dealing with chronic fatigue with her daughter, Nancy, who also has CFIDS.

Nancy Masoner (nm) was diagnosed with CFIDS when she was in middle school. Typical of many children with CFIDS, Nancy struggled with a school system that did not understand her disability. She is now a part-time boarding student at Bryan College in Dayton, Tennessee, and loves it. Unable to read because of the neurological symptoms she has, Nancy does her studying through books on tape.

Craig Maupin (cm) contracted CFIDS ten years ago, when he was a teenager. He currently lives with his family in Crozet, Virginia. He enjoys fishing, music, and computers.

Robin Ralston (rr), challenged by autoimmune illness since 1986, rests at home with her two cats. When she has the strength, she enjoys writing, singing, and helping her husband with his sacred music publishing business.

Christina Smith (cs) has lived for seven years with fatigue resulting from

CFIDS as well as fibromyalgia. In August 1995, she stopped working and moved in with her parents. During the past few years she has focused her energy on getting to know God better by reading the Bible and praying.

Nancy Swinyard (ns) has a Ph.D. in psychology and was working for a contractor to the National Institutes of Health until an automobile accident in 1985 resulted in disabling chronic pain, fibromyalgia, and chronic fatigue. She invests her talents for the Lord in an informal ministry of encouragement to her church in Bethesda, Maryland, and to her family. Nancy lives alone, except for her dust bunnies. She worries when she begins to name them.

Lynn Vanderzalm (lv), with lots of help from friends and family, has survived ten years of living with CFIDS. Her nineteen-year-old daughter, Alisa, who has suffered with the same illness for the same period of time, has been a constant companion in the journey. Lynn and Alisa both have written for journals published by the CFIDS Association of America.

Laura van Vuuren (lvv) was incapacitated by CFIDS in 1994 while serving in Africa with a Christian relief and development agency. A former journalist and researcher, she feeds her continued interest in international work through the ongoing career of her husband, who shares her care for the world's poor.

Amanda Volkers (av), now seventeen years old, has battled CFIDS for over six years. Each day she struggles not only with trying to go to school but also with the many questions she has because of her illness. Amanda's four siblings and her mom all have chronic fatigue and immune dysfunction syndrome.

Further Help with Your Fatigue

If fatigue seriously limits your ability to function, my earlier book *Finding Strength in Weakness: Hope and Help for Families Battling Chronic Fatigue Syndrome* (Zondervan, 1995) will help you find ways of coping with the physical, emotional, relational, and spiritual dimensions of your situation. A fifteen-page resource section at the end of the book lists articles, books, organizations, and support groups that can be of tremendous benefit to you and your family.

If you have questions about chronic fatigue and immune dysfunction syndrome, you can request from CFIDS a free information packet, which will also include an extensive bibliography of useful books and tapes:

The CFIDS Association of America, Inc.
P.O. Box 220398
Charlotte, NC 28222-0398
1-800-44-CFIDS (800/442-3437)
FAX 704/365-9755